OUR
IMMORAL
SOUL

OUR
IMMORAL
SOUL

A Manifesto of
Spiritual Disobedience

RABBI NILTON BONDER

SHAMBHALA
Boulder • 2014

SHAMBHALA PUBLICATIONS, INC.
4720 Walnut Street
Boulder, Colorado 80301
www.shambhala.com

© 2001 by Nilton Bonder

Translation from the Portuguese by Diane Grosklaus.
Edited by Kendra Crossen Burroughs.

Printed in the United States of America

∞ This edition is printed on acid-free paper that meets the
American National Standards Institute z39.48 Standard.
♻ Shambhala Publications makes every effort to print on recycled
paper. For more information please visit www.shambhala.com.
Shambhala Publications is distributed worldwide by
Penguin Random House, Inc., and its subsidiaries.

*The Library of Congress catalogues the hardcover
edition of this book as follows:*

Bonder, Nilton.
[Alma imoral. English]
Our immoral soul: a manifesto of spiritual disobedience/Nilton
Bonder; [translation from the Portuguese by Diane Grosklaus].
p. cm.
ISBN 978-1-57062-882-5 (hardcover)
ISBN 978-1-57062-924-2 (paperback)
1. Soul (Judaism) 2. Sin (Judaism) 3. Man (Jewish theology).
4. Messiah—Judaism. I. Title.
BM645.S6 B6613 2001
296.3'2—dc21
2001042907

In the depths of our hearts, we have always been free men and women, wholly free.
We have been slaves in the outer world but free men and women in our souls and spirits.

—RABBI JUDAH LOEW
The Maharal of Prague (1525–1609)

CONTENTS

Contents

OUR
IMMORAL
SOUL

1 The Immorality
of the Soul

A hen is only an egg's way of making another egg.

—SAMUEL BUTLER,
Life and Habit (1877)

A NAKED ANIMAL

The title of this book is a play on an expression coined by
Robert Wright in his book *The Moral Animal: Evolutionary
Psychology and Everyday Life*. The notion of a "moral animal,"
based on Darwin's theories, implies that our behavior, habits,
and culture are purely an extension of the biological body. The
Darwinian view of human nature strips us bare before the
world to reveal the undeniably animal dimension of our lives.
Confronted with this nakedness, the conscious human animal
can do nothing about it without calling further attention to his
state. Adam and Eve, our closest animal ancestors, were made
terrifyingly naked when they broke with their primeval nature

and gained consciousness. In trying to cover what had been made visible, they only rendered it more obvious. It is in Adam's very shame that God recognizes his nakedness.

No one is naked unless he or she is aware of it. A great paradox is that we cannot claim dignity unless we are truly aware of our nudity—yet nothing challenges our dignity more than the realization that we are naked. For this is a nudity not of gods but of mortals. It is a nudity that can in no way be called natural, either by biblical definition or by common sense; because there is no nudity in nature. The human is at once the most clothed and the most naked of the animals.

Evolutionary psychology exposes the body's most deep-rooted desire: to reproduce. From the body's perspective, human history is a saga concerned with sexual maturation and the drive to procreate; once that is accomplished, the biological apparatus that made it possible is discarded. The age-old questions—Where did we come from? What are we here for? Where do we go from here?—find their answers in the only affirmative commandment given in Eden: "Be fruitful and multiply" (Genesis 1:28). No other commandments were necessary, for everything proceeded by involuntary action in a world without consciousness. The Garden of Eden was imbued with the sense of peace inherent to fulfillment of the inevitable.

For Darwin, this Eden is still with us, but it is transformed into hell by our consciousness, which desperately tries to come to grips with the discovery of our nakedness. For evolutionary psychology, the body is the driving force behind human action and behavior, hidden beneath the clothing of symbols and culture. A moral body creates a world of clothes in order to cover nudity. Yet, naked, we are still visible—perhaps even more visible than we were when no garment covered us.

What evolutionary psychology offers is a modern, scientific way of talking about our nakedness. After all, it was not his soul that Adam discovered as a result of his consciousness but merely his nakedness. Both the Bible and evolutionary psychology recognize that this experience of consciousness produced a moral animal.

Darwin offers valuable insights when he argues that the physiological differences between the sexes account for the social habits and customs of each era. Much of our world is thereby explained. The world is composed of men and women who seek to fulfill their greatest commandment: Be fruitful and multiply. This is the matrix that allows us to understand social reality through history.

Biologically speaking, for the male to optimize his reproductive chances, he must fertilize as many females as possible. The female, however, is limited to one pregnancy at a time, so quality of fertilization becomes fundamental for her. The ground-is thus laid for a social dance that will vary depending upon environmental factors related to the economy, the type of settlement (urban or rural), and so on. The mating habits that develop may be polygamous in nomadic societies or monogamous in a sedentary lifestyle. The female of the species tries to select the perfect male, the one whose strength, health, intelligence, cultural tradition, or wealth ensures the best odds for successful procreation. The male of the species benefits from monogamy by assuring his right to a woman without needing to engage in cruel or destructive competition with other men who might conquer as many women as they want because they excel in one of the areas mentioned above. In order to keep the peace, each generation within each society will seek out the social conventions that best fit its conditions of "supply and demand." Monogamy, for example, demands a sacrifice not only from the male—who "morally" cannot sow his seed among many women—but also from the female, who must content herself with the best seed available from among "morally" unattached men. This pact of sacrifice may be the way that sedentary and urban societies have found to guarantee the greatest degree of social peace.

According to this notion, men look for women who look for men, and each uses his or her own tactics to attain the best possible outcome of the mission to procreate. All the lively glances that are furtively exchanged in the web of a city are driven by this one desire. In the subway, in offices, in classrooms, in restaurants, at church, or at funerals, humans can see each other's nakedness and are constantly measuring their chances of conquering the opposite sex, thereby fulfilling their greatest design in life. In thus carrying out these fundamental orders that have been given to us, we come as close as we can to immortality, which takes physical form in our children and their magical capacity to go on living after we are gone.

We, the naked humans, know this. We also know that apart from the concrete act of procreation, courtship and seduction impregnate us with the taste of life. We know that a happy old age thrives on the laurels of an unwasted life. We know that frustration and depression are by-products of the failure to adequately fulfill this destiny.

There is no heresy in this view. Adam and Eve are naked, and they have a commandment to fulfill, by man taking woman and woman taking man. Consciousness endows them with an awareness of their nudity, and thus humanity acquires the status of a moral animal—a naked animal that sees its own nakedness and therefore needs to cover it before others and itself. All morals, all traditions, all religions, and all laws are products of the moral body, of a moral animal. And all societies are dedicated to clothing our nakedness.

Biblical understanding, however, parts with Darwin and evolutionary psychology when it assigns humanity another animal mission, beyond procreation. For the Bible, in describing the origins of humanity, the order to procreate is the only affirmative commandment. But the Bible tells us of another aspect of human nature that precedes consciousness itself—the impulse to disobey orders. That is why humanity was also given a

negative commandment, a "don't do." The human being is perhaps the greatest metaphor of evolution itself, whose task is to
transgress what has been established.

Even before gaining consciousness and perceiving our
nakedness—that is, before realizing that we are moral animals—we humans had to confront this other dimension of
ourselves, this capacity to disobey for which we were probably
designed. As the Bible makes perfectly clear, this dimension
originates from the purest animal nature—the snake—and
chooses woman as the most favorable means for planting its
seed and passing it along to man, so that together they might
transgress. This partnership in transgression in fact begins with
God Himself, who implants a grain of consciousness by stipulating a prohibition. The difference between evolutionary psychology's view and the Bible's is that in paradise the world of
animals, the world of bodies and anatomies, is not given solely
an affirmative commandment—"Multiply"—but a proscrip-
tive one as well: "God gave the man a commandment, saying,
'You may definitely eat from every tree of the garden. But from
the Tree of Knowledge of good and evil, do not eat, for on the
day you eat from it, you will definitely die'" (Genesis 2:16–17).

It is interesting that when the Creator commands, He fully
exercises His role of defining guidelines for His creations; but
when He prohibits, He opens the door to a dimension of co-
creation. Admitting the possibility that His creatures may do
something they are not supposed to do is tantamount to sum-
moning them to join in creation, by either obeying or disobeying. Notice that obeying a prohibition is distinct from obeying
a commandment. Choosing to obey a prohibition or to transgress against it is an evolutionary act.

For the Bible, the human being—the state-of-the-art animal—is driven not only by physical needs but also by the
impulse to betray those needs. We embrace our body's demands
through a moral effort to clothe a naked body, an animal

body—which simply means that this body's purpose has been recognized. But we also embrace our transgressive, evolutionary dimension. For consciousness, this dimension is not moral but "immoral." It aims to to err, to rebel, to betray. My main purpose in these pages is to explore this transgressive dimension of human nature, which I perceive as representing what we have come to call "soul." In contrast to the popular understanding of the term, soul is defined here as that component which is conscious of the need for evolution, that portion within us which is capable of breaking with norms and mores in order to attain a higher stage of development. The soul is therefore transgressive and "immoral" by nature, for it does not validate the interests of morality.

The biblical text is often interpreted to mean that the soul is an ethereal body blown into a lump of clay by God. This is but one interpretation. Nowhere does the story of human creation state that the human being possesses two essences: one physical and one immaterial. What God breathes into man at the moment of creation is life, which is present not only in the dimension devoted to fulfilling the body's vital necessities—its need to reproduce—but also in the dimension devoted to the need to evolve. What God breathes in is not the soul but matter's organic status. For the Hebrew Bible, there is no duality in human essence. Rather, there is the possibility of choice—between obedience and disobedience.

We should therefore not understand "soul" as an essence distinct from the body. The duality we try to capture through the concept "soul" derives from the human capacity to choose between obedience and disobedience. The soul is part of the body—the part that disobeys. It is the term we use to identify the evolutionary element of the body—the body that, on the one hand, demands our conformity to rigid rules of conduct determined by the very nature of its being but that, on the other, will every so often betray itself and rebuild itself.

This book is about this soul—a soul that was never a moral policeman safeguarding the public order. The latter concern is in the body's interest, for the body is the true Establishment, seeking to maintain the status quo. Much to the contrary, the soul is that part of our viscera whose precise purpose it is to betray these interests.

The codes we carry inside us, impelling us to betray the moral animal's status quo, derive from our awareness of death—the recognition that the same body that desires reproduction also kills us. This, after all, is the fear expressed in the biblical story: that the conscious animals, once they are made aware of their mortality, may desire immortality; for the moral body, the body that recognizes its own nakedness and begins to consciously seek its own preservation, is profoundly mortal. Just as mortal is unquestioning obedience, the equivalent of evolutionary stagnation. Neanderthal man might have died or vanished were it not for his evolution, for his breaking with the integrity of his body in order to fulfill a destiny that must have been deeply distressing and "immoral"—his mutation and transformation. It is only the transgressive soul—that is, evolutionary betrayal of the body's status quo, of the moral body—that affords the true possibility of immortality. In the animal realm we achieve immortality by obedience through reproduction, and morality fulfills the role of protecting this immortality within the realm of human consciousness. Immortality, on the other hand, can be achieved by disobedience through evolution. The immoral soul fulfills the role of protecting this immortality within the realm of consciousness.

In these pages we will examine the imperative immorality of the soul and its ongoing questioning and critique of the body's morality as necessarily the best way to represent our interests. I turn to the teachings of Jewish tradition to demonstrate that our true soul is transgressive. This immorality, which often poses severe threats to the body, is the territory where the human being does battle with God, and out of this clash, a new human being is invented—today's humanity.

TRADITION AND TREASON

Tradition and treason are two inseparable concepts. Tradition (from the Latin *traditio*, "handing over") encompasses the tasks of instinct taken up by human consciousness. Within the realm of consciousness, preserving the species means heeding social teachings meant to guarantee the greater purpose and meaning of our existence: reproduction. Tradition includes three main areas: (1) the family, a structure that has been molded to best meet the reproductive interests of any given socioeconomic context; (2) the social contracts essential to ensuring the best possible conditions for preserving and reproducing life; and (3) the beliefs designed to provide the task of preservation with its theoretical and ideological underpinnings.

The emergence of religious fundamentalism in our day is undoubtedly a legitimate reaction to a world that wants to shift the agenda from collective purpose to individual purpose. Consuming instead of reproducing implies emphasizing reproductive means over reproductive ends. It means placing priority on the present at the expense of the future. It means polluting more than conserving. In short, it means threatening an animal, which will react with all the aggression and desperation of any cornered being.

Treason or betrayal, by contrast, involves transcendence. Abraham betrayed his father and his culture in order to settle a land that was to be his own. Major treason occurs within the realm of family relationships when social contracts are broken and heresies are committed against belief systems. The Bible itself is filled with strange transgressions transpiring in the midst of countless reminders about fulfilling the law. Time and again, the firstborn's right to his father's heritage—a veritable obsession in the Bible—is ceded to the younger child. Isaac transgresses against Ishmael, Jacob against Esau, Rachel against Leah, and Joseph against Reuben.

I must underscore that in these cases there is no failure to fulfill the law but rather a transgression of the law; the Bible legitimizes these attitudes and, in the absence of any reprehension, offers its collusion. To transgress is to transcend, and our history would have no political, scientific, religious, cultural, or artistic martyrs if it were possible to transcend without jeopardizing the survival of the species. Even the thirst for power, which we cast as a great villain blocking the way to an idealized world, is not as threatening to tradition as is betrayal through transcendence. If the thirst for power drives someone to violate the common sense about how to preserve and reproduce our species, that person is an outlaw. The traitor is a transgressor who advocates another law and another reality. When someone goes against the traditional family structure, if he can be characterized as wicked or perverse, his place in society is guaranteed: he represents what shouldn't be done. He has an important role to play, and his privileges are assured so long as he remains in the wrong. His situation is special, and every society has room for a certain number of special cases. If, however, this individual breaks with the family structure and also shows a desire to legitimize his behavior, he will become unacceptable—and a good candidate for martyrdom.

A martyr is someone who dies for the greater good of all of us. Although the way in which the martyr transcends the norm would be unacceptable behavior in everyday life, it is nonetheless a monument to our potential immortality. This is in fact the messianic concept, which seeks to create an emissary of God who is as powerful as God Himself, and who comes to proclaim the commandment to transgress as resolutely and rigidly as the commandment to reproduce. Within the realm of consciousness, the Messiah* is the symbol of the evolutionary animal determination contained in the genetic code itself. It is necessary to err, transgress, and violate the status quo in order to achieve a transcendence that is secretly desired by the very tradition that has been betrayed.

Just as tradition depends upon betrayal, as preservation depends upon evolution, as today's "getting it right" depends upon yesterday's mistake, the opposite is true as well. For evolution is possible only if there is a certain "obedience" that can be challenged or defied.

Of course, transgression is not automatically meritorious. We know that yesterday's heretic may be today's successful product of mutation and evolution, just as he may also be today's cancer. The animal inside us is committed first and foremost to its own preservation, whether that end is best achieved by staying the same or by changing. The catch is that it is impossible to change without running the risk of making an absolute mistake. Over time, the disappearance of a species has been the "mere cost" of many processes of evolution. But movement is inexorable. Mutation is indispensable to continuity, and it can never occur without the tension inherent to this circumstance: the road to health may prove the road to disease. The transgressor greatly fears this realization. He needs tradition and traditionalists to permit his incursions into a given hell or a given paradise.

Traditionalists are horrified when they see one of their favorite sayings contradicted: Yes, we *should* change horses in the middle of the stream! Our desire to establish the perfect conditions under which to execute our task of self-preservation

Messiah (Hebrew, *mashiach*) means "the anointed." According to this traditional Jewish belief, a descendant of the family of King David would rise to the throne of Israel, restoring it to its days of former glory. As time went by, this became a belief that a "leader" would come to redeem the people from their repression and bring them prosperity. As a mythical figure, the Messiah became transformed into a divine representative who would do away with misery and injustice and establish a new society.

finds expression in Genesis in the fear that human beings will want to build their own Eden outside Eden, reproducing the original garden in all aspects but one: the possibility of transgression. We are left with the sad lot of depending constantly upon the transgressor. The Messiah who announces his arrival will always be a martyr, even in the hands of transgressors, for in arriving he will be transformed from king of transgressors to king of traditionalists. Transgressors do not want a traditional Lord, nor do traditionalists want a transgressing Lord. The Messiah is a dream, represented solely by the transgressor who is worshiped and then immediately devoured, so that this world will consist neither solely of what we have to do nor solely of what we should not do. There can be no tradition without betrayal, nor betrayal without tradition, as an animal cannot be whole without evolution, nor can evolution exist unless animals are whole.

Identifying the Immoral Soul

Spiritual discourse has created the concept of soul. This discourse recognizes that the profound experience of existence produces two opposing forces that paradoxically complement each other—and that are also what best equip human beings for the task of self-definition. We do indeed understand ourselves to be the product of a tension between opposites, and this is reflected when we coin the terms *body* and *soul*.

The body is seen as a kind of antonym of the soul; one represents matter and its needs and the other, spirit and its needs. It is when we set out to define this matter that we create confusion about "body" versus "soul." The body is a product of the past, at a given point in time. Its greatest interest is self-preservation, not merely because of the instinct for physical survival but also because of emotional attachment to its own being; for the body is an entity that "likes itself" and that perceives immortality as a

11

chance to achieve eternal preservation. The soul is a demand made by, and inherent to, this body—a demand that comes from the future. What this body may come to be in the future threatens its status quo while seducing it with the promise of an immortality that may be attained by better shaping and adapting the physical form.

Our consciousness grasps these two deep-seated human desires: reveling in the joy of being as the cumulative part that has formed us, and reveling in the joy of being as we exist at a given moment in time. It is true that the soul breeds a complex desire: to attain immortality through transformation; yet what is immortalized is not what we perceive this body to be at a given point in time. The soul immortalizes us, but with a small caveat: it is not exactly "ourselves" that will be perpetuated but rather this change in ourselves.

Herein lies the tragedy of spiritual experiences. All this effort to arrive at an understanding of "soul," all this desire to attain immortality by transforming the self, ends up throwing us right back to the definition of "body." This is why many people see the soul as the assessor of morality, intent on protecting the body from the menacing threats of transgression. It appears, then, that the soul safeguards tradition, when in reality it was conceived to be the safekeeper of betrayal and of evolution. Because tradition so often places priority on the urge for self-preservation, it often would rather take on the body as its enemy than have to confront the soul, which is the real culprit responsible for ruptures and transgressions.

This inversion occurs not only within collective traditions but also within the realm of the individual, transforming betrayed into betrayer and vice versa. I will attempt to show how those who are betrayed represent the pole of conformity, of "settling" for things as they are—they are in fact betrayers of the soul. Traitors, on the other hand, choose rupture—that is, they choose to be the soul's loyal knights.

Evolutionary psychology asserts that the body generates morality in order to protect its self-preservation interests. This morality stands in contrast to the soul's transgressive forces. The soul thus lives off what society labels "immoral."

What we have here is no satanic knot in our perceptions. It is simply that it is hard for us to legitimate actions in our daily lives as either absolutely positive or absolutely negative. We can, however, affirm that wickedness is related to the degree of deceit and dishonesty. Negative things disguised as positive as well as positive things disguised as negative are the real deceiving forces that produce evil. The interests of the body disguised as the interests of the soul, and the interests of the soul disguised as the interests of the body—these are the misleading forces in human life.

It is essential to understand that a constant tension between two diametrically opposed concerns—preserving and betraying—is intrinsic to spiritual life. True spiritual experience gains nourishment from the present moment, which encompasses the tensions of past experience (which is preserved) and of future experience (which we create through betrayal of the past). The importance of the present lies in carrying the responsibility of honoring both past and future—that is, in knowing how to compromise in our commitments toward preservation and betrayal.

Perceiving Issues of Body and Soul

We have seen that laws and the duty to what has been established are the territory of the body. The inexorable law of reproduction is the very definition of *body*. The soul, on the other hand, is characterized by disobedience, as in the act of eating the forbidden fruit. Jewish tradition, however, does not label this action "original sin," which in Christianity implies a corrupt nature inherited by all humankind. Rather than evidence of instrinsic sinfulness, it is simply the first incidence of the inclination to disobey recorded in human consciousness. Adam and Eve were apes until this act of disobedience marked the advent of consciousness and transformed them into human beings. But their act of rebellion grew out of very deep-seated, subtle natural traits. It was an act of disobedience committed not out of disrespect for God but out of respect for something else—human nature or human inquiry; and this is an important distinction.

There are two ways of honoring natural traits that hold true for all living beings, but only human beings have consciousness of this. The human difference is that we are aware not only of our body but also of our soul, of laws and acts of disobedience. We can obey while disrespecting just as we can disobey while respecting. These two possibilities of human consciousness allow us to conceive of the soul, for it is the soul that goes beyond the body's interests to identify acts of disobedience committed in respect as well as acts of obedience committed in disrespect.

The age-old battle between the letter and the spirit of the law reflects two wholly legitimate human perceptions. The letter of the law is consonant with the body; the spirit of the law, with the soul. The latter seeks to prove that disobedience to a law sometimes has more to do with the law itself than does obedience. The Talmud itself—the encyclopedic work on Jewish law created with the stated intention of guaranteeing the preservation of an endangered group, and thus responding to the body's needs—admits that the transgressive element is fundamental to any structure meant to respond to human interests.

Rabbi Shimon ben Lakish states in the Talmud (*Menachot*): "There are times when the setting aside of the law might be the very means of its preservation." Quite subversive in tenor and usually ignored by more reactionary groups, the notion underlying this sentence in fact permeates the entire Talmud. Down through the ages, what has remained valuable about this idea is that it maintains a tension between the intense quest for the literal meaning of the law and the implications inherent in the transgression of any literality. This is why the Talmud has been written in the form of disagreements over legal rulings among the various rabbis. The law is thus defined through the process of argumentation. The text not only records and preserves the rabbis' arguments but also asserts that they may not stand as such forever. The inappropriateness or erroneousness of arguments may be only temporary. Moreover, this erroneousness lends legitimacy to a law (or to a given interpretation of that law) by relieving it of the weighty responsibility of representing an absolute, eternal answer or condition.

The Talmud's famous "minority opinion" approach—where the dissenting voice is recorded along with the view consecrated as law—is not the product of a democratic mentality, as many imagine. Back then, the point was not the right to an opinion, because political and social issues were simply not cast in such a light. The point was that the best and most appropriate understanding is generated through tension. The law—that is, bestowing upon a certain viewpoint the privilege of being called "right"—only gains its legitimacy to the extent that compliance with that law may, under certain circumstances, require disobedience. A law is legitimate only if it contains within itself not merely an interest in preserving itself (its body) intact but also an explicit preference for disobedience (when this implies respect) over obedience (when this implies disrespect).

The law "Do not kill" is not legitimate unless the act of "killing," or of breaking this law, does not on some occasion better express a respect for life than the act of "not killing." Nature exemplifies this constantly, where killing is done with respect for life (namely, the life that is sustaining itself through either hunting or defending itself). We might, for example, argue that in our society and civilization, capital punishment does not best represent reverence for life. However, it is naive to think that under certain circumstances killing cannot better represent the desire to "not kill" than the very act of "not killing." Life will always make manifest that any law can be transgressed, whatever the morals of a given group, time, or place.

Any law that does not admit the possibility of compliance with it precisely through disobedience to it is despotic. In the Talmud, we find an interesting postulate that underscores this concept: unanimity is disqualified. What to the modern, democratic mind would seem the ideal model, the Talmud sees as potentially disastrous. According to the tractate of *Sanhedrin,* when a criminal is tried for capital punishment—which requires twenty-three judges—if the sentence is unanimous, this decision is rejected and the judges are disqualified. This law— an expression of the soul and obviously subversive—is leery of any case that is so well presented that every shadow of a doubt is eliminated. Unanimity reflects accommodation to an absolute truth, and absolute truth, which has tremendous destructive potential, is inimical to life. It is the soul that detects this, for it is the soul's interests that are jeopardized by such unanimity. Public opinion, dogmas, conventions, morality, and traditions can often represent a kind of unanimity that disqualifies their capacity to judge what is fair, healthy, or constructive.

When Right Is Wrong and Wrong Is Right

For everything we understand to be right, there is a "wrong" behavior that, under certain circumstances, may better express this rightness than the apparently "right" behavior itself. According to Hasidic teachings, even the first and most forceful of the Ten Commandments—"I am God your Lord" (Exodus 20:2)—can be fulfilled through disobedience.[1]

The Hasidic lesson begins by stating, "There is nothing in human experience that has been created without purpose." This triggers the question: "And what purpose is served by those who deny the existence of God?" This question in turn implies a more specific one: "Is there some transgression of belief in God that may under certain circumstances prove more constructive than honoring this belief?" The teaching concludes: if a needy person asks for help from someone who believes in God, the believer may respond piously by saying, "Have faith and leave everything in God's hands." A nonbeliever, however, behaves as if there were no one else in this world to whom the needy person could turn—and thus he or she feels compelled to help.

Not believing in God may thus produce the same effect that we expect to come from belief in God. Of course, we might argue that real belief in God should compel us to help the needy, and that is true. But someone who feels responsible for the world because he has disobeyed the First Commandment may in certain situations be better prepared than those who believe. There is no way a guideline can exist unless that guideline can be complied with precisely through noncompliance.

One amazing concept that the rabbis came up with in their efforts to understand human behavior is known as *mar'it ha-ayin*, literally, "what the eyes see." It refers to everyday situations in which a person may be doing something in accordance with religious law, yet others are led to regard the action as illicit. Compliance with traditional Jewish dietary laws has been used to illustrate this concept. For example, Jewish tradition forbids the mixing of meat and milk products in the same meal. We might ask: is it permissible to eat a vegetarian cheeseburger in public, where it might look to others as if one were breaking this rule? Apparently, there would be nothing wrong with that. If there is no real meat involved, only soy products or other substitutes, the law is not being broken.

The rabbis, however, have ruled that such a meal would not be kosher if consumed in a public place, owing to *mar'it ha-ayin*. It makes no difference that there is no meat at all in the

17

sandwich or that even laboratory testing would offer chemical proof that no meat had been eaten in conjunction with milk products—nevertheless, a vegetarian cheeseburger cannot be eaten in public. The rabbis would ban the sandwich because the image of "wrongness" had replaced one of "rightness."

What the rabbis wanted to underscore is that our interactions with others in public influence how we decide whether something is right or wrong. After all, right and wrong are always relative, not absolute. In the eyes of anyone who doesn't know that the person is eating a vegetarian cheeseburger, the act would lead the observer to think the law was being broken—regardless of the truth of the matter.

A phrase from the Book of Numbers (32:22) is often used to prove the validity of this interpretation. Here Moses tells the descendants of Gad and Reuben: "You may return home and be guiltless before God and before Israel." Since the people of Israel are mentioned in the phrase along with God, the rabbis took the verse to mean that it is not enough to be guiltless before God; we must also be accountable to the world.

The rabbis not only defined limits for human conduct within the social sphere; they also argued that what is legal and right is so in a given context. It does not matter that no conventions have been broken; the eyes of society make it so. Thus, the letter of the law (do not mix dairy products with meat) has been exchanged for the spirit of the law (eat kosher food and do not mislead others into eating nonkosher food).

One question remains: if something that is intrinsically right can acquire the status of a wrong, can we imagine a social situation in which something intrinsically wrong can be turned into something right? Remember that these are situations of the soul, where it is no use having your accounts in order in the eyes of the world if you are not guiltless before the Absolute. There is a story of a very poor woman who went to a rabbi with a question: since she didn't have enough money to honor the Sabbath as she would like, she wanted to know which purchase would be more important—the candles needed to usher in the Sabbath at sundown on Friday or the special Sabbath breads over which a blessing is said at the Friday evening meal. The rabbi researched the question and came to the following conclusion: if the woman had to choose between these two items, she should buy the candles, since in the Sabbath ritual these were used before the breads, and therefore they should take precedence. According to legend, a voice immediately came down from the heavens, admonishing the rabbi for not displaying greater wisdom. It was clear, said the voice, that she should buy the breads, for they would provide the nourishment that the poor woman needed. What was "wrong" became "right."

These inverted *mar'it ha-ayin* situations are a great challenge because they imply a total break with conventions and laws. When this happens, we feel we have been affronted aesthetically and culturally. After all, *mar'it ha-ayin* does not see the essence but only the form. What the eyes don't see—for example, that there is nothing unkosher about a vegetarian cheeseburger—matters little compared with what they see. The same holds true when breaking the law is a better way of preserving the letter of the law than the letter itself. But the eyes do not see this and are therefore shocked.

When we grasp this concept in its reverse form—that what the eye doesn't see might constitute true obedience to the law, derived precisely from setting aside the law—we have acquired a new understanding of the soul.

In short, my intention is to reformulate the concepts of body and soul. According to this new definition, the original sin was not an act of ceding to a temptation of the body, as the Christian or fundamentalist interpretation holds. Adam and Eve were tempted by the soul in order to fulfill their design as a creature capable of evolution. The body's only desire was to fulfill the commandment of procreating within the territory of Eden.

The body was sent forth from the Garden by the disobedient side of its nature—that is, the soul—and driven into another territory. In order to survive in this other place, which was not entirely its natural habitat, the body developed a form of protection. This protection devised clothing to cover its nakedness, created the consciousness of birth and death, and invented morals. Whenever the body insists on re-creating Eden—the place where its desire is the only reality—the soul counterattacks with its immorality. In Eden, where there was only one commandment to obey, immortality lay in reproduction. In this new territory, where the body gains awareness of its mortality, the soul becomes indispensable—as its sole immortal part. The soul's immortality lies in the fact that its commitment is to alternatives beyond the body, which under certain circumstances may involve relinquishing the present body for something more appropriate.

UNFAITHFULNESS AND BETRAYAL

If we agree that being human requires us to maintain a tension between body and soul, between tradition and transgression, we are admitting the possibility of two kinds of serious deviations: attachment to the way things are and betrayal of the way things are. Attachment wounds the soul in the same way that betrayal wounds the body. Both are forms of exaggeration or imbalance that breed violence. Violence against the soul is violence against life itself, and as such it leads to depression. Violence of the body turns outward, in hatred and revenge.

Attachment threatens and violates the integrity of a human being just as betrayal does. Betrayal is easy to identify, but we rarely realize the violence we do our souls through attachment. Our greatest problems in life come when these two states—betrayal and attachment—are out of balance. What is most fantastic is that they always occur together.

Betrayal cannot be experienced unless attachment exists. This dynamic merits our attention. When, for the soul's reasons, people are prompted to commit a transgression in their relationships, they will immediately find themselves up against the body's penchant for attachment.

Let us take the case of a married couple. A major imbalance occurs whenever one of the partners takes a step forward in his or her life. This step, which disrupts the settled status quo, should also push the other partner to take a step forward. If this happens, the two partners will remain in balance. However, when a husband or a wife takes a step forward, the most common reaction is for the other one to take a step back. An imbalance is established, and this nondynamic situation blocks the natural process of life.

Most marriages fall into an endless repetition of this reflexive action. When one spouse begins transforming him- or herself—which means the relationship will need to change as well—the other one will often take a step backward by demanding fidelity to earlier commitments. We fail to recognize that rights of attachment are meaningless in a relationship where the explicit commitment is to be *in relationship*. In such cases, the spouse or lover would fail to understand that any demand of loyalty through attachment is ineffective since the explicit commitment in a relationship is to relate to the partner's growth and transformation. If one party in a relationship changes, an agreement must be fulfilled: everyone must get moving. Reacting by taking a step backward—making emotional demands, listing justifications, or claiming rights—represents a form of attachment that constitutes the greatest betrayal of the implicit commitment of caring for each other.

For the soul, attachment to the old is tantamount to betrayal. It is not rare to hear of people abandoning a religious tradition, a career, or even a great passion for some higher calling of the soul, motivated by absolute love and respect. "I betrayed so as not to betray," as the Brazilian saying goes—many traitors have stated this with no real awareness of the import of their words.

According to an ancient practice of biblical times, certain individuals were declared "impure" and thus had to "leave camp." The modern mind understands "impure" as synonymous with "unclean" or "dirty." This is not exactly so. The impure individual was someone who was temporarily unable to participate in the game of life, in point of fact representing both the attached and the betrayed. Examples of the impure cited in the Bible include lepers and those who have been in contact with a dead body. But we might also extend this concept to situations such as that of a mourner. Someone who has lost a loved one oscillates between the despair of attachment to the way things were before and the despair of feeling betrayed by this sudden change of affairs. The anxiety of loss and the inability to conform to the new situation are accompanied by feelings of rejection, of having been abandoned by life, and this leads to depression and anger. These people cannot remain in the camp. They must "go away" until the time when they can return, conscious that they are reentering life's tension between the preservation of the body and the transgression of the soul. Jewish mourning practices require surviving family members to stay at home and abstain from work for seven days, temporarily setting them apart from others and somehow reproducing the biblical idea of leaving camp. Leaving camp was a therapeutic technique that created awareness of an individual's fragility at a moment when he or she was unable to obtain nourishment from life's driving forces—that is, preservation and transgression.

Someone who has been betrayed falls into a subcategory of mourner—although perhaps he faces the harshest kind of mourning. He feels the pain of transgression in his body and the pain of attachment within his soul; for anyone who is betrayed is undoubtedly someone who sins through attachment. By definition, you only feel betrayed if you are grappling with problems of excessive attachment.

The Tension between Good and Right

A particular statement in the Bible is of major relevance: "Carefully listen to all these words that I command you, so that it may go well with you and your descendants, since you will be doing what is good and right in the sight of God" (Deuteronomy 12:28).

This verse addresses the question of existence much as Darwin does. Evolutionary psychology endeavors to understand the greater purpose behind human existence so that it may then ascertain what best represents the well-being of humans. The realization of the purpose for which they were created is what makes living beings feel happy and fulfilled. The Bible speaks in terms of a fulfillment that will make things go well "with you and your descendants." What is it that should be fulfilled? As in the story of Adam and Eve, the Bible has a twofold response: doing "what is good and right in the sight of God." We need to understand not only what it means to do what is "good" and "right," but also the relationship between the two.

One possible interpretation is that the tension between what speaks to the soul (good) and what speaks to the body (right) must be respected. Neither "good" alone nor "right" alone can fuel the everlasting spark that moves and motivates everything in life. We are "well" when we perceive that the tension between good and right (in the sight of God) is balanced

in our lives. "Good and right" often means that "good" will weigh more heavily than "right"—meaning that right is betrayed in the name of good. At other times, good will be betrayed in the name of right—as we saw in the example of the vegetarian cheeseburger, or as occurs in any process of *mar'it ha-ayin*. The concept of *mar'it ha-ayin* in fact represents the workings of our own culture, which lays out a moral code for the body in order to ensure stability. It does this by creating a pole to serve as a reference point in establishing the necessary tension between good and right that is essential to the attainment of well-being.

The reactionary stance insists that there is an absolute good and right for every situation. The revolutionary stance argues that good and right are irreconcilable. From less radical perspectives, the art of living involves understanding when "good and right in the sight of God" may mean good more than right or right more than good. For those who view life from the angle of this tension, all human existential discomfort is the product of an imbalance. To reiterate: this tension is not a question of equality but of relationship. As in a game of tug-of-war, the rope may be pulled in one direction (good) or the other (right) at a given moment or may be pulled equally by the two opposing forces—but what matters is maintaining the tension. It is when a loss of tension, a loosening, occurs that disharmony sets in. Whenever we opt for more good than right, the tension disappears, and the result is guilt and violence. Whenever we opt for right over good, likewise causing a loss of tension, the result is attachment and depression.

Maintaining this tension is a challenge not only in relation to oneself but in relation to someone else. The secret lies in knowing that what is at stake is not a struggle between good and right, nor between soul and body, as the culture once believed. What is at stake is the tension and close relationship and dependence between good and right and between soul and

body—or, better put, between morality and immorality, preservation and rupture.

A Definition of Betrayal

If we take the previous discussion into account, we will discover that the word *betrayal* is a wild card. It expresses a loss of tension. We betray when our choice causes a loss of tension either because we hurriedly opt to defend good over right (or vice versa), or because we hurriedly relinquish good over right (or vice versa). Betrayal can thus be propelled by faithfulness or unfaithfulness, by attachment or detachment.

Betrayal is a kind of measurement, and it is not always easy to understand measurements. Take acceleration, for example. You can't "see" acceleration. What we can discern visually is speed. A car may be moving up a hill even though negative acceleration is occurring. We watch the car ascending, but the movement is in a way one of descent, which would be revealed in the measurement of velocity. We may likewise imagine human situations in which betrayal is a form of measurement.

While certain marriages appear to conform to norms of fidelity, they contain movements of betrayal that underpin infidelities that will occur later on. By "infidelity" I mean not just the breach of commitments but also the honoring of commitments when honoring them is destructive. We all know when our lives are undergoing positive acceleration, or when we are moving at an artificial speed because acceleration is negative. We feel depressed when acceleration becomes negative, even if speed remains positive. This is what I am referring to as a loss of tension.

We can detect this process quite clearly in one of the most intense aspects of human interaction, the sexual act, and in sensuality in general. We cannot afford to lose tension between good and right in these interactions. If we do, we are overcome with fear and self-consciousness, and we lose touch and presence. We can opt to hold good above right or vice versa at certain moments, but we cannot lose the tension between the two. The loss or preservation of this tension is easily perceived during these moments.

We can interpret a relationship of sensuality as a process in which—since we try to hold to both the good and the right in the sight of God—we find ourselves standing before life itself. Any betrayal will be noticed immediately, and this betrayal becomes a kind of measurement for all interactions. Those involved no longer see speed but only acceleration. Any slack or looseness is noticeable—in other words, the partners can concretely recognize situations of betrayal. A look, a sigh, a gesture, a movement—and we know whether this tension is present or mechanisms of betrayal have taken hold.

Intimacy provides an x-ray of the relation between body and soul and reveals states of tension or lack of tension. This is why intimacy is so provocative, for it immediately reveals when we are betraying or not.

The concept of betrayal has three inseparable facets. It refers to the nonfulfillment of previously established conventions or agreements; it has to do with the nonfulfillment of expectations; and it concerns precise information about a person's intentions.

Someone who betrays is inarguably someone who exposes his innermost desires and intentions, but contrary to what we generally imagine about betrayal, it is quite difficult to betray openly. Although the behavior of a traitor is often seen as weakness, betrayal actually requires great courage, because when the betrayer exposes himself, he reveals intimate secrets.

The act of betrayal never shifts the focus of relations from the area of intimacy. To the contrary, the pain caused by betrayal derives from a deepening of intimate experience. Norms and conventions can be used to avoid change to such an extent that one might have no other way out but to betray. When this is done, much of what is being avoided is exposed. This is what is so hurtful for those who have been betrayed: being led to depths of intimacy that they would rather avoid.

I am not talking about someone whose infidelity comes from attachment. This might not be an experience of deepening intimacy—to the contrary. "To betray" does not necessarily mean to leave a relationship through infidelity. This type of betrayal may hide deep-seated processes of attachment, in point of fact representing an act of betrayal of the soul. I am speaking of betrayal here as a measure of how the tension of life is broken. Infidelity might well be a form of escapism that does the very opposite: it helps mantain the lack of vital tension in life.

Traditional Models of Betrayal

BETRAYALS OF CULTURE: ADAM AND ABRAHAM

Let us research our primitive understanding of the human being by relying on the oldest story in the Bible: the Creation. The Book of Genesis speaks of three stages in the creation of humanity: Adam, Abraham, and Jacob. Each of these three archetypes is associated with an important moment in the evolution of the story recorded in Genesis. Adam represents a break with nature; Abraham, a break with society; and Jacob, a break with the family.

Adam transgresses when he discovers that, unlike the other animals in the Garden, he is faced with not only the absolute purpose of reproduction but also a prohibition that must be obeyed or disobeyed.

Abraham—to whom God promises progeny as numerous as

the stars of heaven and the sands of the seashore—is the man who inaugurates history. This focus on him and on the "multitude" that will descend from him is a clear option to tell history through a story. But what is so special about this man that he was chosen to found a nation? Like Adam, Abraham was a transgressor. His personal story begins when he hears an order: "Get out of your country, and your birthplace, and your father's house, to the land that I will show you. I will make you into a great nation" (Genesis 12:1–2). The verb "get out," which is in an emphatic form in the original, implies "break with"—in other words, betray.

Jacob is one who commits a transgression against someone else. He represents the betrayal of personal relationships within the family. He steals his brother Esau's birthright as firstborn son, committing grave treason against his father and his brother. He takes advantage of his father's blindness—not unusual in situations of betrayal—to appropriate the blessing that was meant for Esau, and with the help of his mother (symbol of good), he breaks with his father (symbol of right). His flight and the suffering provoked by this betrayal initiate an exemplary process: the establishment of the first family. It is this family that will be "potent" enough to found the twelve tribes of Israel and represent the true "multitude" promised to Abraham, the social transgressor.

Earlier, we looked at the first example of betrayal: the evolutionary traitor who discovers that not only rules may be transgressed but the game itself. Now let us look at the second case—the social traitor—to help us gain a better grasp of the act of betrayal and the immorality of the soul.

Abraham's story begins with a rupture. The Bible tells us nothing about his childhood, probably because it is not of great relevance. This becomes important to our focus on Abraham's initial act and how it relates to what is so special about Abraham. Leaving behind his culture and his past for the sake of the future means knowing how to reconstitute the tension between body and soul, learning to make this break in light of the demands of the future and not just the demands of the past.

This is the "chosen" status that is proposed to Abraham and his multitude in the form of a pact, or covenant. Traitors usually like the idea of being a "chosen one," because it seems to compensate for the fact that society sees them as "deviants." From the perspective of the body, someone who "gets out" of his father's house is not a model to be emulated. Yet from the perspective of the soul, he is. The notion of a "chosen one" is the soul's interpretation, while the body sees it as something dangerous, requiring immediate corrective action.

Michael Lerner, in his book *Jewish Renewal*, offers an enlightening interpretation of Abraham's act of breaking with his "house" in order to begin the search for a "new house." According to Rabbi Lerner, the question raised by Abraham's saga is whether or not we can break with the violence of the past. All of us have constructed the notion of "body" through conditioning imposed from our past. Our parents (particularly when considered from the analyst's couch); our experiences, from which we glean "certainties" and a fear of the unknown; and our culture, which indicates what is "right" and sees this right as "good" by definition—all imprint our destiny on us. It is this destiny that Lerner sees as the violence of the past. The proposition that we ought to remain the same and never leave our "father's house" is more than indecent: it does violence to a person. To remain the same means that we keep on doing what was done in the past. If we were unfortunate enough to be abused by our parents, we will be much more likely to repeat this with our own children. How many times did we have to suffer hearing our parents say, "*I* had to put up with such-and-such—why can't *you*?" Here is an educational concept where the past is surely the determinant of what is right and good.

The son who makes the break, who does not take up his father's profession or his culture, is not the doctor his parents dreamed of but a musician, a deformed mutant, because he listens to the demands of the future and is detached from the past.

Abraham was not what his parents dreamed of. Knapsack on his back, off he went in search of his own land. Prototype of the "bad child," Abraham questioned the violence inherent to the inevitability of his destiny.

But what lends special import to Abraham's decision to transgress, to leave home, is the test to which life puts him later on. The real question is not whether Abraham will manage to break with the violence of his father's past but whether he will manage to accept this as a behavioral attitude toward life and therefore refrain from imposing violence on his own child. In other words, did Abraham take up his search for good, in detriment of right, solely for his own purposes, or did he inaugurate a transforming process between generations? If the answer to the latter question is yes, then Abraham ushered in a history that is not merely cyclical and repetitive from generation to generation but which, when each one of these generations breaks with its past, opens the way to a future grounded on the needs of the soul and not of the body—a future that belongs to the mutant and not to a body preserved as is. It would not be the land of our grandparents but a strange land, a land that is in strong tension with the land of our memory, which constitutes our "house."

Was Abraham to social reality what Adam was to evolutionary reality? Was Abraham to the option for evolution within the social realm what Adam and his transgression were to the option for evolution within the realm of nature? If so, then the future would be different from the past. The violence of the past would be filtered out of the future and a new social being would be possible. The concept of reaching a messianic future depends upon the human possibility of transgressing against what is right, of transcending the house and territory of our past.

The test came. In an atmosphere reminiscent of the betrayal committed in his youth—when he was told, "Get out of your country, and your birthplace, and your father's house"—Abraham hears a new order, similar in structure: "Take your son, the only one you love—Isaac—and go away to the land of Moriah [the Temple Mount in Jerusalem]; and offer him there as a burned offering on one of the mountains that I will designate to you" (Genesis 22:2).

It was evidently the practice in that region that a father should offer his firstborn son in sacrifice. As a good citizen of Canaan, Abraham obeyed the design of his culture. It is interesting that the same God of transgression is now the God who speaks for culture. Abraham's experience when he receives this order is identical to the first occasion, and the question is whether Abraham will be able to perceive the hidden hook. The God of the soul now speaks in the same tone and in similar fashion, hiding his true identity—as the God of the body.

Abraham walks with his son. His inner doubt is terrible: should he do what is right as if it were good, without questioning it? The denouement of Abraham's moment alone is awesome. He does not obey the original order. Neither does he disobey it. Abraham hears God say something different from what He had originally said. Instead of "Sacrifice your son," he hears, "Do not harm the boy. Do not do anything to him" (Genesis 22:12). Abraham does not disagree with God but learns to hear a different order from the same God. Here the divine figure is symbolic of the deepest understanding of what life, of what reality, expects of Abraham, who betrays neither God nor himself; instead, he legitimates his transgression as being God's true will. Abraham's secret lies in this nonrebellion, where good is practiced to the detriment of right, ushering in a new morality—the morality of the body, whose mutation was a product of the soul. Abraham proclaims his faith in the demands of the future and, therefore, of the soul. He is immoral, for he legitimates a different morality, which springs from the same source as the morality of the past.

It is only at this moment in his life that Abraham closes the cycle, not passing on to his son the violence of his morality and culture. In Abraham's relationship to his father's generation, we only know that Abraham has perceived his path—to leave home—but it is when he is faced with the possibility of having to offer up his own son that Abraham is choosing to see his son live in another "house" and another "land." As his legacy, he leaves Isaac a new world, where the nonsacrifice of his firstborn son represents the search for a land that does not belong to his contemporaries or compatriots. Abraham is disobedient. Within the social realm, he stands not only as fulfiller of the positive commandment to become "father of a multitude" but also of the negative commandment to transgress the expectations, or violence, of his generation.

Abraham learns not only to opt for the "good" but also to decree it as the new "right," the one that will replace the old and "betrayed" right. There is no treason in this action, and the tension between past and future, between body and soul, is restored. Were it not for Abraham's ability to hear God express a divine will that differed from what had originally been ordered, he would have failed to recapture the perspective of the body, and a loss of tension would have occurred. Abraham would have been betraying by choosing the soul without achieving reconciliation with the body. His mistake would have been no different than if he had obeyed the initial commandment and enforced the violence of his generation. In this hypothesis, in addition to opting for the body to the detriment of the soul, Abraham would not have truly left his home.

This point is very important. Leaving home does not just

mean abandoning a body that belongs to others—it is the act of abandoning one's own body. Transgressing our own convictions is essential. It is like the case of a law whose legitimacy depends upon the hypothesis that under certain circumstances disobedience is the best form of compliance. For Abraham, being absolutely human—fulfilling what is expected of us—means accepting the hypothesis that the best way of preserving his integrity may lie in relinquishing this same integrity.

Abraham establishes the possibility of a new law, a new understanding of orders—he opts for the immorality of the soul. From the perspective of the body, this immorality is what allows the evolutionary process to take place, where the new order is always legitimate. The fact that Abraham waited to hear this new order means he recovered the lost tension and eliminated any risk of committing a real act of betrayal.

We can see that Abraham could also have decided to make a new "good" fit the old "right," sacrificing his son and coming to peace with himself by finding a convincing justification that he had done a "good" thing. But Abraham couldn't do that; his solution had to be finding a new "right" for this "good."

Abraham is consistent and allows his son to find another "house" or another "land," just as he had—the promised land of which Abraham had dreamed, a land whose tradition includes ruptures. With the founding of a new religion, one that recognizes the soul's transgressive nature, a better future became possible. Abraham enjoys a cathartic moment, for he understands how wonderful the future can be if we legitimate our transgressions.

BETRAYALS OF FAMILY: THE STORY OF JACOB

The third archetype is Jacob, the one who transgresses within the realm of the family. He does not betray his nature or the violence of his society; his specialty is betraying "the Other."

Jacob represents the transgressions that all his children and descendants will repeat. Let us not forget that it was Jacob who received the name Israel and that the twelve tribes of the Jewish people were descended from his twelve sons. Jacob's betrayal and transgressions were to have a profound effect on the historical destiny of the Hebrews, inaugurating a process that transcends the individual.

The Bible uses the question of firstborn rights for symbolic purposes. Being the firstborn child meant inheriting the family name and history. The firstborn was the chosen one who would ensure continuity and carry on the future. Jacob breaks with the law of the firstborn, as does his son Joseph—an action that has become the stereotype of the Jew. Down through the ages, powerful and domineering peoples who came to view themselves as the legitimate heirs of civilization's history in a certain generation have labeled the Jews usurpers of the rights of the firstborn.

What, however, is Jacob's model? Abraham had made a break in his past and did so again at the end of his life. He legitimized betrayal by hearing in a new way, one that was more compatible with what he perceived as good. Jacob's experience was similar. He stole his brother's birthright and fled. His theft is only legitimized decades later, when he and his brother are reunited.

This reunion is preceded by a struggle with God. In a mysterious account at the end of Genesis 32, Jacob finds himself alone, facing the night, before his reunion with his brother. He's afraid of his brother and anxious because he stole his inheritance. A being then appears and wrestles with Jacob throughout the night. Struggle—a word that denotes tension—is the process of instability in quest of a renewed balance. The being proves to be God. In prevailing in this struggle, Jacob receives the name Israel, the meaning of which is recorded in the text: "you have struggled with God and with men, and have prevailed" (Genesis 32:28).

Jacob represents the act of opting for a new "right" in his relationship with his peer, with the Other. But it is not simply a matter of his stipulating the new "right" for the identified "good." Jacob cannot do the same as Abraham, who heard God retract His order. God is not going to ratify the new "right" with new words. The alternative is to struggle with God and with men so that the new "right" will prevail. This hand-to-hand struggle, which begins as a fight between men, in the end proves to be a dispute with God. Doubt is not eliminated through deep self-examination and self-betrayal, as was the case with Abraham. Doubt is eliminated by showing the courage to assert a new "right," to betray the Other, and legitimize oneself in the process.

Abraham is like the father who accepts his musician son and dances with him, recognizing that his dream of a medical career for his son is not the right that best fits what is good. Abraham does not merely tolerate; he dances with his son, who goes off in quest of his own land. Jacob is the brother who follows the life of the artist and intellectual, leaving the presidency of his father's companies to his entrepreneurial, administrative brother. Jacob is the one who will have to legitimize his choice, resolving his own doubts and gaining the maturity to realize that he is the true heir. This heir is, of course, not the heir of the body, of companies and assets, but the heir of the soul, of the deep-seated desire to venture forth in life instead of following well-traveled roads.

The complications that ensue when we break with a peer or a brother are what cause the Other to see this as a betrayal. The traitor threatens the person who preserves his body. Legitimizing the Other's right to be an artist, recognizing that this is a valid option, means questioning yourself about your own ignored potentials. For someone who preserves and protects the body, this doubt causes a pain that can often result in violence and accusations of betrayal.

Jews carry this stigma. As questioners, they have been looked upon with suspicion by the Christian world—a world that inherited this civilization but that feared its brother, the "usurper of inheritances," because his mere presence stimulated profound doubts.

The Jewish people occupy a dangerous position in the Western world. In a sense, the Jews are examples to the world, for in deeming themselves chosen and seeking a new land lost long ago, they are exploring questions of the soul. This is why the Jews provoke a strong reaction from the world of the body.

Later I will explore how Christian tradition set itself the task of making Judas the prototypical Jew. A traitor from the cradle, the Jew is the most vivid example—and one never replicated in the history of civilization—of treason and betrayal.

From the perspective of the Jew, of Israel (Jacob)—the one who fights with God and with men—it is not easy to legitimate the position of "chosen one" without resorting to violence. The challenge is to wholly legitimate the new "right," not with arguments or justifications but through a deep belief in the soul and its transgressions.

Betraying Yourself

A Hasidic commentary puts an interesting spin on an apparent slip of the tongue. In Exodus 7:9, God tells Moses to demand that Pharaoh free the Israelites from slavery and foretells that Pharaoh will counter with a challenge: "When Pharaoh speaks to you, he will tell you to show yourself something that surprises you" (that is, a miracle). The rabbis are quick to ask, "Shouldn't Pharaoh say, 'Show me something that surprises *me*'?" They answer their own question by explaining that the very clever and experienced Pharaoh has asked the right question. If Moses merits respect, he must show that he is someone who surprises himself, not someone who surprises others.

The ability to surprise oneself is in fact the greatest proof of a person's power. To surprise others, we merely make use of tricks we have already mastered. To surprise ourselves, we must be magicians, transforming the "I" we thought ourselves to be. As Brazil's greatest landscape architect, Roberto Burle Marx, put it: "In the creative process, the problem is not when we copy others, but rather when we start copying ourselves."

The hero of the body is he who surprises and seduces others. His power lies in making use of the past and wielding his skill as a magician. Things that have already been done, said, seen, spoken, and heard become instruments for surprising others. But the hero of the soul is he who surprises himself, and his powers derive from what has yet to be done, said, seen, spoken, or heard. Rich with the potentials of unconventionality, the future is this hero's instrument of power. The ability to betray ourselves to ourselves and to surprise ourselves with ourselves is the source of great strength. While the body rejoices in the conquests of seduction, the soul rejoices in the conquests of wonder provoked by surprise.

The greatest moral failings are not temptations of the flesh but sins of the soul. The seductions of the absolute, of aesthetics, purity, certainty, and authoritarianism, are conquests of the body's morals and tradition. It is, however, sin that elevates the soul—as in the case of Adam and Eve's transgression. Once again, there is nothing satanic about this—it is simply the soul's perspective. For the surprises that are caused by the relative, the unfinished, the limited, the mixed, the mistaken, the spontaneous, and the sinful strengthen the soul and afford its prime nourishment: evolution.

Steps toward Betrayal

A fascinating Hasidic teaching posits four ways in which the body may react in response to the soul's demands. Developed by the late Lubavitcher Rebbe, this teaching focuses on a paradigmatic episode of the meeting of the interests of body and soul: the moment when the Israelites flee slavery in Egypt. Symbolizing an active movement to escape slavery and attain freedom, this event offers a fine opportunity to exemplify human processes aimed in a similar direction.

It should be underscored that Eden is symbolic above all because it represents a place that once was good but is no longer. Our analogies gain even greater depth if we note that the Hebrew etymology of the word for Egypt—*mitzraim*—means "narrow place."

At some point in life, all of us find ourselves in a place that has grown too narrow. Places that once served the purposes of development and growth become constrictive and confining to us.

In narrating this piece of Hebrew history, the Bible provides a fascinating account of how the Israelites extracted themselves from a confining place—though in the process they came up against a wall as real and as deep as the ocean itself. The Pharaoh, regretting his decision to let the Israelites go, pursues them with his army and then pushes them back against the sea. Finding themselves caught between the most powerful army in the world and the waters, the Hebrew people turn to their leader Moses in desperation. What shall they do?

When we decide to leave a tight space, a similar process occurs with our body: it doesn't want to leave, for it doesn't like change. The sensations of constriction and discomfort are what eventually convince it there is no other way out. But where should it go, when the body knows nothing beyond itself? The soul, with its immoral proposal to dislodge the body, forces the body down a path where it ends up facing an apparently insurmountable barrier. How can it move toward the "promised land," toward the future, if there is an absolute chasm—an ocean—lying between the present and this future? So the body questions the soul's good sense. The doorways of the past close, the doorways to the future are not yet open, and the body experiences the worst of all sensations: the panic of death.

Trapped between the army and the sea, the Hebrews—representing the body—can assume one of several attitudes. According to the Hasidic teaching, there are four classic behaviors; that is, when people are unsure of how to proceed, they will divide themselves into four "camps." The first group wants to go back, the second wants to fight, the third wants to cast themselves into the sea, and the fourth takes up prayer.

From the soul's perspective, all four of these attitudes are forms of the body's resistance. The very idea of "making camp" is in itself a way of coming to a halt. Going back means recognizing how strong the confining space is; it has become such a powerful habit that we feel we were carried away by the illusory dream of leaving. Everything was wrong from the beginning, and the idea of returning implies going back to a narrow life that conforms to reality and its limits.

Fighting means believing we can make a narrow space wider. If this confining space has imposed itself as a powerful reality, we feel all we can do is challenge it—as if this narrowness were external rather than a relationship between our external and internal worlds. We must never forget that this narrow place was once not so narrow.

Casting ourselves into the sea is an act of desperation. It means giving up the body upon discovering that the soul has positioned us in an unbearable limbo, where the past that defined it no longer exists, yet neither is there a new future to redefine it. In the quest for a new "good," a new "right" is not found, and the only way out is to pay the price of having rebelled against the "right" of the past. From this despair is born resignation: though there is no return to the confining space, a new, broader place will never be reached.

Praying is a way of attempting to make the new situation

into a reproduction of the narrow space. In an apparent resolution of the demands of the soul, the body calls out for reality to be compassionate with it, so the new place does not force the body into redefining itself. The new place is the old one, but without the feeling of constriction. Many of our imaginings about life after death fall into this category.

The beauty of the Hasidic interpretation lies in its use of Exodus 14:13–14, the verse that sketches the reactions of Moses, leader and representative of the soul's interests (entrepreneur of the exit from this tight space): "But Moses said to the people, [1] "Do not be afraid. Stand firm, and see what God will do to rescue you today; [2] for the Egyptians whom you see today you shall never see again. [3] God will fight for you, and [4] you have only to keep still."

This interpretation offers an answer to each of the four camps. To those who wished to throw themselves into the sea: "Do not be afraid. Stand firm." To those who wished to go back: "You shall never see them again." To those who wanted to stand and fight: "God will fight for you." And to those who chose prayer: "You have only to keep still." None of these four camps represents the future and the way out. All represent variations of hesitation and vacillation. They are the boundary where the body dies in order to be reborn into another body with the same soul—on the other bank of the waters.

If none of these attitudes is appropriate, then what is the way to proceed? Let us not forget the reality that interposes an ocean between one body and another. God's answer to the body's vacillation—the answer that comes from the source of every soul and of all future—is at the same time incisive and intriguing: "Tell the Israelites to go forward" (Exodus 14:15).

Go forward or proceed toward what? To where? What obvious solution is this that God is presenting, when none of the camps—none of the body's perspectives—can find a way out?

We know how the biblical account ends: with the parting of the seas. But according to the Midrash (a collection of allegorical commentaries by the rabbis), this parting of the waters transpired in a very specific way. A man by the name of Nachshon ben Aminadav, prince of the tribe of Judah, who didn't know how to swim, began to enter the sea. The waters did not part at first. It was only when he was in up to his nose that the waters divided.

Unlike those in the camp who wanted to throw themselves into the sea in an expression of hopelessness and disbelief in the future, Nachshon understood God's recommendation to go forward. The future exists if you will go forward. However, the future is not linked to the present by the body; the soul is the guide down the dry path through the midst of the waters, from one body to a new one or from one bank to the other. Knowing how to relinquish this body in faith that another will take shape is knowing how to take the step that will lead to where the bottom drops out from under us. As long as we have ground beneath us, we will be stuck in our camps.

This profound act of trust in ourselves and in the process of life is what ensures our passage through the void, which magically turns into ground beneath our feet. What did not exist before now exists, and a new, ample space has become accessible.

We know this process through our birth. At a certain point in time, what had been the most wonderful, coziest place in the world, filled with nutrients that feed the body's development, becomes too narrow. No longer big enough, our mother's womb has become a *mitzraim*, an "Egypt." Exiting dry in the midst of the waters is difficult, requiring a courage that can be found only if soul and body go forward hand in hand. Learning how to give in to the contractions of a too-narrow space, to move toward a roomier space, is a frightening, overwhelming, and magical process.

Arriving on the other shore, elated, we see that the soul exists beyond the body's anatomy. The past has become a new present—the future conquered.

Once on the other side, for a while the body will forget that no place can be big enough forever. Narrowness is a condition of life, and the immoral soul is a mechanism as innate as the reproductive moral body. Eden became a narrow place and, as happens from time to time, the human species perceived the narrowness of its being and of its nature. Undergoing a process of mutation successfully means breaking into a new body, which we did not know could contain our new self.

When to Betray

In his book *Choice of Pearls*, the eleventh-century poet and philosopher Shlomo Ibn Gabirol names four distinct stages involved in recognizing that a space has become too narrow. There are those who (1) know and know they know; (2) know but don't know they know; (3) don't know and don't even know they don't know; and (4) don't know but assume they know.

The first person is at the same stage as those who made camp before the sea. He is awaiting his chance to cross. He recognizes the new "good" and waits for a new "right" that fits it better.

The second person must be awakened. The place is narrow, and he knows it, but he cannot see any way of moving toward the future. Underwritten by the past, the present is so strong that he cannot see beyond it. In these circumstances, the body cannot feel that it is trapped and must go forward.

The third person doesn't recognize that the place has become narrow. He needs urgent therapy to explain away the feeling of anxiety that comes from not knowing what is so wrong about the way he perceives his body.

Nor does the fourth person recognize that his space has grown too small, even though he seems to acknowledge the fact and claim that he is ready to take measures to change it. For him, this tightness is an abstraction, which means he does not really understand the different slaveries to which he is being subjected. Without a doubt, this is the hardest situation to deal with. The breadth of this person's theoretical thinking creates the illusion that he is right beside the sea. But since he has never truly realized how tight the space is, he has no way of moving forward through the sea. The dry path will never open, for those who fail to realize that their space has grown too narrow cannot move forward. No body relinquishes its interests in the name of the soul unless it is deeply aware of its discomfort. This fourth case speaks of a new "right" but fails to fashion a new corresponding "good." And having a new "right" without having a new "good" in sight increases confusion and perplexity.

When the body finds itself in a narrow spot, and when it is aware that its discomfort is caused by this narrowness, it becomes possible to make camp in front of the sea. From this unsuitable, anxiety-provoking place, we look toward the horizon. Reaching it will be no longer a process of the body but one of the soul. It is here on this bank that you "give in" and divest yourself of everything, revealing not only the body but changing it as well. This metamorphosis frightens us, as we think we may be relinquishing our integrity and our very identity.

2 *The Soul's Logic*

If it is the soul that makes us cross from one bank to the other and from one body to the other, and if it is the soul's immorality that makes the seas part, then we must get to know its "logic." As we become familiar with this logic, we will recognize elements within ourselves that do not belong to the body which seeks to preserve and reproduce itself, but that derive from a deep inner guide that tells us to transgress.

Many of the concepts and parables I draw upon in these pages have been handed down from Hasidic tradition, whose greatest merit lies in its desire to preserve based on betrayal and transgression. Its wisdom comes from having the good sense to recognize the legitimacy of the body and its interests while always subsuming the latter to the interests of the soul. As good descendants of Adam and Eve, how could we not taste of the forbidden fruit and how could we not leave home?

PEACE TO THOSE WHO COME FROM AFAR

The prophet Isaiah said, "Peace, peace, to the far and the near" (Isaiah 57:19). In the Talmud, this verse is seen as curious since it inverts the logically expected order: "to the near and the far." Why does distance come first and proximity second? Why not the other way around? In the third century, the rabbis Abahu and Yohanan engaged in a fascinating disagreement. They recognized that the prophet was not speaking of geographical distance. Rabbi Yohanan, representing the perspective of the body, argued that "near" and "far" referred to a person's proximity to sin; therefore the prophet was first blessing those who remain far from sin, and only then does he bless those who are near it. Rabbi Abahu, on the other hand, argues from the perspective of the soul, affirming that those who come from afar have covered a long road of error in order to reach this point. "Near" refers to those who have had little chance of "surprising themselves"; they have had little experience traveling the byways of the soul.

For Abahu, the prophet first blesses those who come from afar, because his respect is aimed specifically at those who have not settled or conformed, namely, at the transgressors. In order to reach what is right for this moment, these people have risked many false "rights." Nevertheless, since they are extremely loyal to what is good, they have always been pursuers of what is right. Put another way, in order to perceive what is good for a given moment, they have placed their stakes on many false "goods," but because of their extreme loyalty to what is right, they have nevertheless always pursued good.

THE SHORT LONG PATH OR THE LONG SHORT PATH?

Rabbi Joshua, son of Rabbi Hanina, said: "Once a child got the better of me. I was traveling and found myself at a crossroads. Then I saw a little boy and asked him the way to the city. He replied, 'This is the short and long way, and this is the long and short one.' I took the short and long one, and soon ran into gardens and orchards, which were truly insurmountable obstacles. When I went back, I complained, 'My child, didn't you tell me this was the short way?' He retorted, 'But I did tell you it was long!'"

On the path of survival, routine is often the short way, the simplest way, but it is the costliest and therefore the longest. Taking the simplest, shortest route is an evolutionary law. Bodies inarguably move in the closest, shortest direction. Branches reach for light and animals seek water, but their inner intelligence—their souls—remain alert to long-term changes. The struggle to survive takes place on the battlefields of the short world and of the long world. Those who travel short paths that turn out to be long run the risk of extinction. Surviving species are the ones that know how to choose the long short path.

In our everyday lives, we know full well which are the short processes and which are the long ones. We often opt for shorter paths. But we also possess mechanisms for detecting whether the path is a "long short way" or a "short long way," allowing us to redirect our lives, in relation to work, love, and friendships.

Courage lies in heeding the little child at the crossroads who alerts us to the two possible paths. This child is the soul. We should not be scared off by parables of devils in disguise standing at crossroads. When we reach a crossroads, the devils are the ones who want to point out the "shortest" way. Someone who warns us that short paths may prove long and long paths prove short is not a demon.

After all, crossroads are vital. They are not just places where we choose a road but places where we choose to survive, and the long short path may lead us nowhere. If you find yourself at a crossroads, remember the little boy and be careful lest your body seduce you into taking a short path. Remember that peace belongs first to the one who comes from afar.

WHY SACRIFICE?

Rabbi Bunam was asked: "What is meant by the expression 'sacrificing to idols'? It is unthinkable that a man should really bring a sacrifice to idols!"

He said: "I shall give you an example. When a devout man sits at table with others and would like to eat a little more but restrains himself because of what the people might think of him—this is sacrificing to idols!"[2]

This teaching begins by questioning the logic of the expression "sacrificing to idols." If we realize that they are idols—that is, empty, illusory, and devoid of any real meaning—how could we possibly make sacrifices to them? Rabbi Bunam's answer is that we do this more often than we imagine—whenever we believe that something abstract or material can be gained through behavior or attitudes that constitute sacrifices to nothing. How many of our efforts and sacrifices are in fact "offerings" to nothing? Who needs our restraint or our abstinence? Does God have any need of our "moral" acts that seek to hide our nakedness? Didn't God realize immediately that Adam had eaten from the Tree, precisely because he donned garments to hide his nakedness? When he clothed himself, Adam made an offering to a god of nothing—the god of his moral animal.

We must understand that the god of the moral animal, of the body, is not always *god* with a small *g*. For it was God who said, "Be fruitful and multiply." But we can never be careful enough, because much is done — or not done — as a sacrifice to nothing. How many people could we have "called out to dance" in the course of our lives, but we didn't because we were making a sacrifice to nothing? We sacrifice to the god of shyness, of shame, of fear of rejection. How many times should we have said no instead of wearing ourselves out by feigning virtue in offering to idols: to the god of expectation, the god of envy, the god of guilt?

We should not fear what others may say or think. We should not fear our own self-image, which is the prime altar for idolatrous sacrifices. How many opportunities have we let slip by because it wasn't "appropriate" for us to do one thing or other? Our self-image, like our morals, is an instrument of the body that cannot see itself in "another" body — that is, in a different way of being than the one to which we are attached.

Rabbi Bunam warns us to be cautious when it comes to abstinence and deprivation. Often enough, instead of demonstrating respect for life, abstinence may well represent a way of worshiping smaller gods. The body is responsible for an intricate network of psychological negotiations to preserve us as we are. But we have been made to believe that our body is constantly tempting us with its desire—when it is the soul that will not settle for the body's meaningless sacrifices, and it is the soul that is responsible for boldness, daring, risk-taking, and transgression.

BETTER BETRAYAL THAN HYPOCRISY

To the Maggid of Koznitz came a man who, in order to mortify himself, wore nothing but a sack on his bare body and fasted from one Sabbath to the next. The Maggid warned him:

"Do you think that the evil urge is keeping away from you? It is tricking you into that sack. He who pretends to fast from Sabbath to Sabbath but secretly eats a little something every day is spiritually better off than you, for he is only deceiving others, while you are deceiving yourself."³

The Maggid wants to rip away the veils of hypocrisy. Those who fool themselves are worse than those who fool others, because the one who fools others is more likely to realize he is doing so than the one who is fooling himself.

Betrayals grounded on fidelity can be much more violent than betrayals grounded on transgression. This is not a generic prescription but one possibility we must always bear in mind as we go through life. In marriage, for example, we tend to measure the "health" of fidelity in terms of adultery. How many marriages are profound betrayals of the promise to seek a life of mutual emotional enrichment? To continue in this type of marriage after all efforts to mend it have failed is a much more serious betrayal of the soul than any act of adultery is a betrayal of the body—where by "body" we mean the past and our commitments of the past. Hypocritical fidelity is a commitment to the past that blocks the present and the future. It may be an option but it is idolatrous.

I am not defending adultery as a solution, just as the Maggid did not recommend that we eat secretly while pretending to fast. But hypocrisy disguised as exemplary behavior is more pernicious than adultery, and its various consequences will be just as harmful, or even more so. Much emotional illness, dysfunctional behavior, and domestic violence is a consequence of the act of fooling oneself.

According to evolutionary psychology, the moral code of monogamy—like other sexual behavior patterns—developed as a way of better guaranteeing the reproduction of a given group. Modern Western civilization has deemed the prevailing family model to be the best guarantee of social peace, since it is believed to help reduce the tensions inherent in reproductive competition. The behavior of the moral body—responsible for this status quo—must be continually monitored by the soul to make sure the former is not inadvertently acting against its own best interests. For the soul, the tension created by transgressing against culture itself raises new possibilities and alternatives that find much greater support in true betrayal than in hypocrisy.

The immoral soul is constantly committing acts of sabotage against the established order. Its role (which implies great risks) is essential to our remaining faithful to life. When it comes to real-life situations, the transgressor is more welcome than the hypocrite. The transgressor does more good to his or her body than does the hypocrite. But the body cannot accept this, since its role is to clothe rather than undress. Its desire is to procreate, not betray.

The moral animal masks its intentions in order to guarantee what it believes to be the best way of preserving itself. It is hard to defend the immoral soul before society. This is why so many religious traditions have inverted the biblical proposal and have taken up a different role: that of safekeepers of the moral animal.

The spiritual proposal, however, is clear: better the betrayer than the hypocrite.

Better a Passionate Rebel Than a Conformist

When he was young, Rabbi Moshe was vehemently opposed to Hasidic teachings. One time when he was staying with Rabbi Asher—who likewise opposed these teachings—they received a Hasidic prayer book. Rabbi Moshe grabbed the book and threw it to the ground. But Rabbi Asher picked it up, saying: "After all, it is a prayer book, and we should not treat it with disrespect!"

When the Rabbi of Lublin, who favored the Hasidic movement, heard about this incident, he commented: "Rabbi Moshe
may yet join Hasidism [which did eventually happen]; Rabbi
Asher will always be an enemy. That is because he who burns
with passionate hatred may someday burn with passionate love.
But the path of someone who is coldly hostile will always be
blocked to possibilities of encounter."

The Rabbi of Lublin clearly knows how to unveil the innermost reality. Even though Rabbi Moshe's attitude appeared
more intolerant on the face of things, his willingness to pas-
sionately reject what "after all was a prayer book" discloses the
possibility of encountering a new moral body, and a new way
of being toward oneself. Such is not the case with Rabbi
Asher, who has become rigid in his way of understanding the
world. Even though he apparently obeys a "moral" code of
conduct, he in fact disrespects it, for deep down his sentiments
are the same as the other rabbi's, much as he acts with outward
respect.

What is radical about this perspective is that once again
the role of spirituality and the soul is perceived as going
against culture, insofar as culture represents the conformist,
moral aspect of a society. The biblical postulate concerning
the transgressions of Adam, Abraham, and Jacob (Israel) re-
inforces the mission of those committed to this postulate:
neutrality must constantly be overridden—either the place
has become too narrow and must be dealt with accordingly, or
we are still at the stage where we do not recognize its narrowness. Not yet having crossed the sea, not having become the
new man he will eventually become, Rabbi Moshe has made
camp and is fighting against barriers and crossroads. Rabbi
Asher "doesn't know" but "thinks he knows." To the world, he
appears to behave more gently, when in truth he has the
potential for even greater violence than the traitor, because he
is a hypocrite.

TRANSGRESSION AND GROWTH

Rabbi Nachum of Chernobyl once said: "I have a greater fear of good deeds that appease me than bad deeds that horrify me." Human experience alternates between states of alertness and states of sleep. We constantly construct ourselves based on the camps we pitch and the camps we abandon. Rabbi Nachum wants to underscore how important it is to be horrified, because it is a sign that we are growing aware of a tight place. Those with no sense of horror lose the ability to detect narrowness. When there is no break with convention, when so-called good deeds breach none of the moral animal's codes, we simply become more insensitive. Whenever we do what is expected, we reinforce our state of sleep, our pattern of automatic behavior. We have an inner tendency to want to please ourselves and those around us, and to obey our culture's morals.

As a result, we are gradually lost to ourselves. To awaken is to be able to perceive horrible situations within our lives, in both the private and the social and cultural realms. A new way of being can be born from this sense of horror, which can lead to a new form of family, of property, and of tradition. Conceiving of family, property, and tradition as immutable constitutes a desperate attempt to deny human nature, which, as it mutates, constantly demands fresh forms of morality.

In transiting between one moral standard and another, the human being unclothes himself again and, now awakened, is reminded of his soul. The Maggid of Mezritch referred to this awakening when he said: "A horse that knows itself to be a horse is not a horse. This is the human being's arduous task: to learn that he is not a horse."

The soul can be perceived in the act of awakening and in feeling the sensation of horror. In both cases, the soul occupies itself with rebuilding the past. For the past, however, the soul is always immoral and dangerous.

COMPATRIOTS OF THE SOUL

In Psalm 119, the psalmist says to God: "I am a sojourner on the earth; hide not Your commandments from me." Concerning this verse, Rabbi Barukh said: "He whom life drives into exile and who comes to a land alien to him has nothing in common with the people there, and not a soul he can talk to. But if a second stranger appears, even though he may come from quite a different place, the two can confide in each other, and live together henceforth, and cherish each other. And had they not both been strangers, they would never have known such close companionship. That is what the psalmist means: "You, even like me, are a sojourner on earth and have no abiding place for Your glory. So do not withdraw from me, but reveal Your commandments, so that I may become your friend."[4]

People who engage in transgressions of the soul are regarded by others as aliens and outsiders. If you make a radical change in your career, develop a new relationship, give up a bad habit, overcome your fears, or make a break with the status quo, you will experience a loneliness that only someone else who is familiar with these experiences can understand. The nature of the experience itself may be quite different, but you will become partners insofar as you are both strangers.

Howard Polsky adds: Make your own path. This may take you into exile and your native society may become foreign, and you may have very little in common with the people from there and have no one to communicate with. But do not forget that you will always have God to help you find others in exile with whom you will have much to talk about.[5]

God is an outsider's best friend, for God is by definition the great Outsider. As the monolithic symbol of the human soul, God is a wanderer, never to be found definitively in any "moral standard." A constant transgressor of conventions and norms,

God is the steadfast friend of the alien and of anyone who follows his own path no matter how much it may diverge from a given community's moral consensus.

It is the person settled in his ways who is indeed alone in the world, for he has come to a standstill in relation to life while everyone else has shifted. The person who has settled will always feel the panic of loneliness, for even an accomplice in conformity is a potential "traitor" of the ideals established by the body. The traitor moves through life with greater assurance and at each spot, each port, each city, or each village will find a stranger to keep him company, someone with whom he can play dominoes.

THE MISSING SELF

Rabbi Hanokh told this story:

There once was a man who was very stupid. When he got up in the morning, it was so hard for him to find his clothes that at night he almost hesitated to go to bed when he thought about the trouble he would have on waking. One evening, he finally made a great effort, took paper and pencil, and as he undressed noted exactly where he put everything he had on.

The next morning, very pleased with himself, he took the slip of paper in hand and read: "Hat"—there it was, he sat it on his head; "pants"—there they lay, he got into them; and so it went until he was fully dressed. "That's all very well, but now where am I myself?" he asked in great consternation. "Where in the world am I?" He looked and looked, but it was a vain search; he could not find himself.

"And that is how it is with us," said the rabbi.[6]

When a place has grown too narrow, we can no longer control the world from the outside. To try to transform a narrow place into a wider one is to attempt to change the world rather than change ourselves. In undertaking this insane task, we end up losing ourselves. The human being's overriding desire to procreate—the moral body's commandment—does not suffice to tell us where we ourselves are. Our compulsory task to procreate is like putting on all our articles of clothing and yet still finding ourselves naked. It didn't matter how much Adam covered himself up—his nakedness grew more and more apparent. Not being able to find oneself stems from an inability to sustain transgression. Living by the book—the manual that tells each one of us what we should do—is not an adequate response to our "self." This is why past generations who have already been through life can offer us no more than teachings about fulfilling what should be fulfilled and disobeying what should be disobeyed.

Wise old people warn us about what we should take to heart while at the same time laughing at the seriousness and rigidity of youth. Finding oneself—a secret that elders try to reveal to the young—means building identities and then casting them off. In many rites and traditions, initiation is much more a moment when betrayal is addressed than a celebration of the educational process of fulfillment. The young adolescent is often called to a place of religious ceremony or to a test of courage more to be reminded that he or she is a "potential traitor" than a compliant custodian of norms meant to preserve a given culture. It is hard for us to see this, for the discourse of religious tradition is often inverted: rather than initiating the soul, the purpose is to initiate the adolescent into the dangers represented by the soul.

When a son or daughter leaves home to follow his or her chosen path, it is a cause for celebration—precisely because the child is betraying so many of our ways of being parents. But the process demands such a huge self-sacrifice on the part of the parents—so that the children are not sacrificed—that parents prefer to turn the meaning of the event inside out. They celebrate compliance, because they cannot accept the bitter reality that their children will find themselves only if they do not merely know each item of their clothing but know as well who they are inside. Without his soul, even Adam clothed is a naked man—a frightening naked man, because he does not recognize himself. Only God can see through the mask to recognize the symptom of a body that fears being itself.

The Book of Ecclesiastes, one of the most important treatises on the nakedness of human reality, warns that there is "nothing new under the sun." At the same time, the future can emerge only from that which has never before happened—the transgression of a present or a past. How are we to take this statement from Ecclesiastes? It in fact contains no contradiction, for transgression itself is as old as human history. That which is not yet will come to be under the sun only when we relinquish obedience—not obedience to others, but obedience that we demand of ourselves, or the obedience of others that we introject as if it were our own.

Brother Satan

Western tradition's inversion of things—wherein tradition is presented as defending the soul when in fact its aim is to preserve the body—causes an important figure to emerge from our subconscious: Satan. His origin can be traced to Hebrew folklore, but his so-called satanic or evil nature is a Western invention. As originally conceived, the name Satan implied an "obstacle" to life or something that misleads. This force was at first understood simply as a limitation, but the notion of Satan began gaining strength as a symbol of "temptation" or as an external unsettling power within life's course. With the Christian tradition, Satan came to symbolize the very idea of "traitor," a force that surreptitiously seeks to lead us into sin.

Satan wouldn't be so important if the issues he brings up were not precisely the great human questions. When it comes to matters that instill great doubt or involve the breaking of patterns, norms, or expectations, we will always see the presence of the satanic figure. He tempts an individual with the possibility of relinquishing something "right" for the sake of something "good"—precisely what I posit to be the soul's task. Satan, however, is cast as an exaggeration or exacerbation of risks that will prove destructive or evil. Let there be no doubt: there is a very real possibility that the soul can become destructive without the body. The true Satan is thus a soul with no body.

The figure of Satan has nevertheless been handed down by culture and tradition as the body's greatest weapon against the soul and transgression. Much has been done (e.g., the burning of "witches") or not been done (out of fear of "demonic" temptation) because the soul has been mistaken for Satan itself.

Religions that try to win over the masses depend heavily on such simplified models of reality. It is easier and more convenient to associate Satan with the risks of change and rebellion than to recognize his connection with conformity and acquiescence. For if Satan is the product of a soul that has detached itself from the interests of the body, then Satan is also present as a body that has detached itself from the interests of the soul.

The Baal Shem Tov once asked his disciple Rabbi Meir Margaliot: "Meirle, do you remember that Sabbath when you were just beginning to study Torah? The big room in your father's house was full of guests. They had lifted you up onto the table, and you were reciting what you had learned?"

Rabbi Meir replied: "Of course I remember. Suddenly my mother rushed up to me and snatched me from the table in the middle of what I was saying. My father was annoyed, but she pointed to a man standing at the door. He was dressed in a short sheepskin, such as peasants wear, and he was looking straight at me. Then all understood that she feared the evil eye. She was still pointing at the door when the man disappeared."

"It was I," said the Baal Shem. "In such hours, a glance can flood the soul with great light. But the fears of people build walls to keep the light away."[7]

Satan is the very trouble we have distinguishing light from darkness. Often, light is to be found neither in what brings preservation nor in what brings transformation. Because of interests that are natural to culture and morals, our society decided to make Satan into a scarecrow to frighten us away from change. Fear of Satan is another tool for keeping people preoccupied with their own norms, not allowing them to dare to discover new possibilities. The language and image of Satan have become a spokesperson for the immutability of tradition, family, and property. His eloquent speech, rich with examples from life and reality, is powerfully paralyzing.

The worlds of fears, of divisions, of defenses, and of control are products of this discourse of human consciousness that demands conventionality.

A Jew from Kossov, who was known to be opposed to the Hasidic way, once came to Rabbi Mendel (a member of the movement) and complained that he was about to marry off his daughter and did not have the money for her dowry. "How much do you need?" asked the rabbi. It came to a few hundred gulden. Rabbi Mendel opened a drawer in his desk, emptied it, and gave the money to the man.

Soon after, the rabbi's brother learned what had occurred. He took the rabbi to task, saying that whenever something was needed in his own house, he said he had no money to spare, yet now he had given such a large sum to an adversary. "Someone was here before you," said Rabbi Mendel, "and said exactly the same thing, except that he expressed himself much better than you."

"Who was it?" asked his brother.

Rabbi Mendel replied: "It was Satan."[8]

The soul is spontaneous, while the body is cautious. The eloquence of the body's justifications is the source of so many needless proscriptions. One of Hasidic tradition's great secrets when it comes to dealing with the body's stances is to employ short tales instead of elaborate arguments. This weapon is implacable when used against the hesitation and vacillations derived from caution.

Rabbi Hayyim Halberstam of Zanz explained why such anecdotes are so efficacious: "If you believe these stories, you are a fool. If you don't believe them, you are wicked." The vessel that conveys information in these brief tales is not discernment or reasoning. To the contrary, it is the paradox of allowing yourself to be caught up in the stories without believing them (understanding them as a figurative expression, so you are not a fool), yet at the same time not disregarding them (not considering them imaginary or illusory, so you will not be considered wicked).

Foolish or Wicked?

This is one of the most perplexing choices human beings face: to be foolish or to be wicked. Nobody wants to be either. To be a fool means harming the interests of the body, of the moral animal. The best way to ensure the most appropriate conditions for procreation and continuity of the species is by not being foolish. An animal that is competing for territory, food, and mates neither wants nor can afford to be foolish. Morals clothe a human being so that he is able to refrain from being a fool while at the same time not exposing himself as a bad person who is concerned only with his own selfish interests. Social rules allow us to be minimally foolish, so that our competitiveness is as civilized as possible. To whom is this civility of interest? To all of us, since it hides the origin of this interest, which is our effort to not be foolish. The better organized a society—offering the fewest possible risks in competition, without making fools of people—the better the society.

Humans know that in the process of avoiding foolishness they can become wicked. To be wicked is to betray the immoral soul. Creating conditions that best foster transgression and transformation implies not being wicked. Wickedness means placing our long-term survival at risk. In order to avoid being wicked, we must give up instant gratification, and that causes us to see our choice as a foolish one that does not benefit us. The more we try to avoid foolishness, the closer we come to being wicked. It is only by breaking with or transcending certain social and moral conventions that one can be less foolish without being more wicked.

Mediocrity: The Horse's Path

Maimonides based his work in the field of ethics on what he called the golden mean. Maimonides considered this middle way of moderation between extremes to be the perfection of human sensitivity.

In total opposition to this assertion, we have the viewpoint of Rabbi Menachem Mendel of Kotzk. When asked why he was so radical and extremist, the rabbi pointed to the road and said: "Do you see? The two sides of the road are for human beings; only horses travel down the middle!" For the Rabbi of Kotzk, the way of moderation is the "horse's path."

Although in theory the middle way seems more balanced and mature to us, the way of the Rabbi of Kotzk is right in terms of the soul. After all, what human being, if powerfully motivated or inspired by longing for the sacred, can help being passionate and extremist? How can we be deeply in love and yet moderate? The horse's path represents the attitude of someone who fears the radical experience of breaking out of a pattern and disregarding the expectations of the majority.

Rabbi Adin Steinsaltz warns that Maimonides' way is not only the mean between extremes but is also the merger of these extremes.[9] The golden mean is not the midpoint; it can be experienced only by adhering to an extreme. In certain situations, the golden mean may coincide with the horse's path, but whereas the latter fears and avoids controversy, the golden mean confronts and profits from it. Following the golden mean implies having the ability to maintain a healthy relation between the differing perspectives of the moral animal and the immoral soul. Following the horse's path means settling for the known, the secure, and the conventional.

Following the horse's path means seeking right without good or good without right. It means failing to recognize that life takes place in the tension between these two quests. This mediocrity that endeavors to evade tensions is just as harmful to the individual as to the species. In the medium and long run, this kind of behavior will lead to great destruction and will place survival at high risk.

Mediocrity means remaining settled in your camp, refusing to recognize the existence or legitimacy of the sea that is there to be crossed. Convinced that he is not being a fool, the individual who sticks to a pitched camp finds his consolation—though he is haunted by the fear of being wicked.

Facing Wickedness

In our imagination, wickedness is one of the forms taken by the waters that hinder our crossing. Whenever we feel, "I can't do this," we become paralyzed, and this makes us pitch camp. We mustn't "hurt someone" or "behave immorally" in relation to our background and education—the body uses such arguments constantly. But there is no way we can get to the other side of the sea without confronting the possibility of our own wickedness.

The Rabbi of Ger said: "We are told by the psalmist first to leave evil and then to do good. I will add that if you find it difficult to follow this advice, you may first do good, and the evil will automatically depart from you."[10]

One of the main secrets in crossing the sea is to refrain from looking at our chances of "doing evil." If we cannot manage to control reality enough to feel certain we are not being bad, perhaps we should listen to the Rabbi of Ger's advice: seek good, and what is evil will be obliterated in the very process of doing good.

Whenever we find ourselves in a situation where a given right must be traded for a new right because we have caught sight of a new and important good, we will find ourselves facing wickedness. But this wickedness is a way of seeking good (and not paying too much attention to "doing evil") from the moral perspective where we find ourselves. The new right to be established will play the role of making what was formerly seen as "bad" prove the best way of not being foolish.

Life will judge us not only for the "wickedness" we believe we can avoid but also by the "foolishness" we allow ourselves. The masters of spiritual traditions—those who devote themselves to comprehending the needs of the soul—are not at all concerned with wickedness. Their greatest concern is foolishness, that is, the idolatrous sacrifice of vitality because we fear judgment by ourselves and others. They will always side with transgressors and disdain those who do not dare to cross the seas.

Using a commonplace occurrence, Rabbi Mendel of Vorki provides this example of the masters' behavior:

It was the day before the New Year, and people from all over had come to Vorki and gathered in the house of study. Some were seated at tables studying; others who had not been able to find a place for the night were lying on the floor with their heads on their knapsacks, for many of them had come on foot.

Just then Rabbi Mendel entered, but the noise made by the
men immersed in discussion at the tables was so great that no
one noticed him. First he looked at those who were studying,
and then at those lying on the floor. "The way these people
sleep," he said, "pleases me more than the way those others are
studying."[11]

Honest sleep was greater than honest learning, and even
though a rabbi considers learning a better "right" than sleeping,
this rabbi knew enough to prefer the "good" expressed in such
honesty. For him, there was no doubt that the "wickedness" of
those who were sleeping was irrelevant compared to the "foolishness" of those whose learning was devoid of meaningful intent.

SATISFACTION AND HONESTY

The Rabbi of Lizensk said: "When someone is no longer satisfied with his business or profession, this is surely a sign that he
is not conducting it honestly."[12]

This correlation between satisfaction and honesty is vitally
important. When forms of hypocrisy creep in and our conduct is marred by pretense, we no longer feel satisfied in our
work, relationships, or other areas of life. In a love relationship, for example, the intimacy that finds expression in spon-
taneity and honesty between the partners produces
satisfaction. People feel satisfied precisely when they manage
to harmonize what is right for them with what is good for
them. Dishonesty reflects the inappropriateness of what is
right or what is good. In order to be honest, your obedience
and your disobedience must be in order. This state is inarguably unstable and shaky. That is why it is so hard for us to
be honest, for the conditions underpinning such honesty are
being constructed at each and every instant.

In this sense, closing contracts between individuals is quite risky. There are moments when contracts may be drawn up, because they represent a convergence of what is "right" and "good" for two individuals. But the constant redefinition of what is right and what is good does not permit contracts to endure unless they are constantly redefined. Rabbi Bunan was once asked to clear up a question about the biblical text in which Abraham makes a treaty with the Philistine king, Abimelech (Genesis 21:27). The questioner said, "It is written that 'the two of them' reached an agreement. Why say 'the two of them'? Isn't that redundant?" Rabbi Bunan replied: "I believe they came to an agreement and made a commitment, but they did not become 'one'; they remained 'two.' "

Many contracts end up creating two different perceptions of the same commitment. These differences can be manifested in how "right" or even "good" is understood. Considering that there are "two" parties in a contract, the possibility that dissatisfaction might arise between them is great, and this automatically entails dishonesty. Betrayal is the consequence of trying to maintain this contract, since the tension between right and good is lost and, as we have seen, whenever this happens, some degree of betrayal occurs.

From the perspective of the body—which is committed to preservation—betrayal is perceived as the greatest crime, a breach of what is right. From the soul's point of view, betrayal is merely the step that fosters change and mutation and that reveals the need for a new good and the subsequent quest for a new right.

What we must always remember is that when we do not feel satisfied (and this sensation is quite easily perceived), we are by definition being dishonest. This correlation has profound implications, and the soul depends upon it to mobilize and sensitize the body.

THE NEED TO TRANSGRESS

Rabbi Elimelech once asked his disciples: "Do you know how far it is from west to east?" When no one ventured an answer, the rabbi went on: "Just one turn around."

Transgression is a process, and the moment when we turn in the other direction marks a new phase in our individual and collective histories. The body and its set of morals, however, perceive this act as "disorientation." Transgression is nevertheless necessary.

Rabbi Bunan warns that the "sins" committed by a person are not his worst crime. The real crime is when someone can "just turn around" at any time but doesn't.[13]

For Rabbi Bunan, the issue is neither time lost nor absurdities committed in the past—the issue is *now*, the present moment, in which we may miss the opportunity to change our course. The failure to transgress jeopardizes two things: the quality of life and its very continuity.

The quality of collective life is jeopardized whenever we fail to exercise our full transgressive potential. Life could be better and bring greater satisfaction, but people abstain from their rights, and in so doing they affect everyone else's rights.

A rich man once came to the Maggid of Koznitz. "What are you in the habit of eating?" the Maggid asked.

"I am modest in my demands," the rich man replied. "Bread and salt and a drink of water are all I need."

"What's the matter with you?" the Maggid reproved him. "You must eat roast meat and drink mead like all rich people."

Later, the Hasidim asked him the reason for this odd request. "Not until he eats meat," said the Maggid, "will he realize that the poor need bread. As long as he himself eats only bread, he will think that the poor can live on stones."[14]

If you don't use your full life's potential, you are in some way diminishing everyone else's potential. If we were all braver and less afraid of being wicked, this would be a better world, one with fewer unnecessary proscriptions.

Every needless proscription is a limitation, and as such it decreases a species' chances for survival. The soul's task of undoing these proscriptions is just as fundamental to the evolutionary process as reproduction and the need for obedience.

When it comes to our ability to better adapt to the world, the soul is our great tool. The soul finds new goals for life and in so doing strengthens individuals and the species, increasing our chances for survival.

In his old age, Rabbi Israel observed: "There are *tzaddikim* (saints) who, as soon as they have accomplished the task appointed to them for their lives on earth, are called to depart. And there are those *tzaddikim* who, the moment they have accomplished the task appointed to them for their lives on earth, are given another task, and they live until that, too, is accomplished.[15] This new task, which extends existence and continues life, is the ability to reorient oneself in life. Taking a "turn around" and finding new tasks, or new "goods," means receiving new vital strength. It is through the soul that these tasks are known. Whoever has the courage to face up to them will not know depression.

Take, for example, the case of people who have fulfilled their "task" of having children and providing for their needs. What is to be done when the children have grown up and gone off on their own, and the parents are some fifty years old? How are they to spend their thirty-odd years or more of remaining life—in effect, another entire life to be lived? Many people discover that their survival depends upon new tasks. Some untie the bonds of past contracts; some manage to renegotiate them. But those who don't do so, who don't use their souls to create new tasks, reduce their chances of survival.

This is true both for the individual and for the human species. The ability to betray a commitment to tasks that have already been accomplished and to create new tasks—defining the species' relation to its environment—is a renewal of the right to exist. This is why we procreate, and it is also why we are mutants. Mutation extends our resident visa in the society of life, because life itself is the chance to define tasks for ourselves.

The soul's logic reveals the transcendental nature of the spiritual quest. This transcendence also has to do with culture and morals. The rebelliousness incited by the spiritual quest makes the soul a tool for breaking with norms, patterns, and paradigms.

Tradition is the codification of principles that allow human beings to understand reality around them and thus improve their odds of doing what is expected of them. These expectations no doubt include preservation of the species, but they also include fulfillment of the mission established by our potential. Tradition contains within itself the human being's great existential conflict, requiring constant negotiations between these two poles of preservation and change. Our history is marked by controversy, and our territory has become the arena of this bloody dispute between the current good and another potential good that will only come into existence when we abandon the former.

Tradition's difficult task of serving as a compromise between the past and the demands of the future makes it fertile ground for betrayal.

3   *Betrayal in the*
Judeo-Christian Tradition

The most important model of treason and tradition can be found in the history of relations between Judaism and Christianity. Western history affords no example richer in symbolism than the episodes that made interactions between these two religious traditions a battlefield for efforts to reconcile body and soul, morality and transgression.

If we take an analytical look at how the facts surrounding the birth of the Christian tradition and its discourse are usually understood, we will discern an interesting relationship between tradition and betrayal. In this book, I have chosen to explore the discourse of Christian rather than Jewish tradition because (1) Christianity's "founding passion" is replete with situations of betrayal and (2) Christianity incorporates Judaism into its mythology and theology, while the opposite is not the case, at least not as directly. Christianity is more present in the mind of the Jews—who have lived through centuries of disputes, controversies, and persecution—than it is within Judaism itself. Exile, for example, which has perhaps been Judaism's most meaningful symbolic element during the two-thousand-year course of this relationship, has not been attributed theologically to Christian tradition or even to the person of Jesus himself. Exile is a broad concept in which Christians have an important historical role to play, but they are assigned no causality or particular symbolic value.

What is the Christian perception of the Jews who remain alive at the dawn of this new century? Despite a vast amount of historical information that has been uncovered and despite the development of greater tolerance, the Christian collective imagination still perceives the Jew as a traitor. The Jew remains the macabre figure labeled as God's assassin. Jewish morality— that is, the Jewish notion of right—was unable to accept the new good brought by Jesus, preferring instead to cling to the old morality, which has grown quite removed from this new good. Jews are therefore corrupt and indecent, for this is how we see those who preserve notions of right that no longer fit reality. The Jews went so far as to choose the liberty of a criminal and to condemn a just man whose intentions were pure. In terms of the morality of the body, of law, and of tradition, Jews are born traitors. Many believe that the very origin of the word *Jew* can be traced to Judas, the traitor.*

---

*Jew (derived from *yehudah*, "grateful to God"): a citizen of the tribe of Judah. The last of the twelve tribes of Israel to maintain its sovereignty, Judah is the origin of all Israelites who have maintained their identity down through history. Jesus himself was a member of the tribe of Judah and thus a Jew—a *yehudi*. At that time, Judas (or Yehudah, the same name as the tribe) was very popular as a first name. It was an easy step from personifying Judas Iscariot as the very image of a Jew, or of a Judean, to stereotyping Jews as traitors or informants.

The extremely captivating atmosphere that surrounded the events of Jesus' life finds expression in the sentiment of passion. In the sense of "suffering," passion is a particular reading of life that evokes an expectation of reciprocity, faithfulness, and justice that often ends in processes of betrayal. This betrayal is at the same time made of disappointment and disillusionment as well as transformation, revolution, and renovation.

It is interesting to note how the Christian view of Judaism frames the Jew as representative of the body, ready to use all means to thwart the transgression of the soul proposed by Jesus and, symbolically, by Christianity. A "new heart," to use the language of the Hebrew prophets (Ezekiel 18:31, 36:26), was refused by their Jewish descendants. This "new heart" was the soul's transgressive proposal, without which a better future—a life characterized by the messianic dream of better days to come—would never arrive. Jews are seen as representing immediate interests: money, idleness, and bodily gratification. Incapable of sacrificing their moral animal, Jews prefer to stick to their camp pitched beside the sea and crucify anyone who declares himself willing to cross the waters; they place the law above love. Ceding to the temptations of inertia and conservatism and of their diabolic fears, the Jews are seen to have impeded the construction of a better world and of a future they could in no way accept.

Even though they tortured the body of the founder and the first of these people of "new hearts," they were unable to sacrifice his soul. This soul endures forever, haunting the body and morals of all subsequent generations, of all "Jews" who have wanted to impede the construction of a network of solidarity and compassion between human beings, putting an end to the iniquity of indifference and injustice.

Commending Jesus' body into God's hands in the name of all souls is the sacrifice that we each should be capable of making out of faithfulness to our soul. Jesus dies for everyone and is resurrected for everyone. Unlike Abraham, father of a multitude and the very promise of fertility, Jesus is celibate and gives birth not to bodies but to souls. Father of all souls, martyr for the soul's sake, Jesus stands in contraposition to the Jew—the latter a staunch advocate of animal morality, of tradition, of property, and of the establishment (the family).

This is how the Jew is portrayed, sometimes under the label "Pharisee," which has come to mean someone who would obstruct the arrival of the new good.

THE FIRST BETRAYALS

The birth of Jesus was the first sign that intense, passionate forces had been unleashed in the relationship of "right" and "good." At the time of the Roman invasion of Palestine, the Jews made an important change in their laws. Observing patrilineal rules up until that time, where rights, titles, and identity passed from father to son, Judaism became matrilineal—in other words, Jewish identity was to pass from mother to child, not from the father. For a Judaism grounded in a patriarchal biblical text, this radical new right in terms of the law demanded some new and very significant good to justify such a change with so many ramifications.

The switch to the matrilineal model occurred because of the Roman invasion. Perpetrating violence against the vanquished, the Roman legions were famed for something quite common during invasions, particularly at that time: rape. For the Roman army, by seizing the vanquished nation's daughters, symbolically conquered the nation itself.

This betrayal of the family, the usurping of bloodlines, and the seeding of Israel's wombs by another people constituted an outright attack on survival. Forcing these wombs to bring Rome's children into the world went beyond the simple pillaging of Israel's present and obliteration of its past—it meant taking possession of its future.

The matrilineal model was the legal solution for determining the status of these children whose fathers were not of Israel; it guaranteed that the children would represent the continuity of a people who refused to be subjugated. Especially in cases of rape, where the offspring would be deemed bastards, a new symbolic understanding of this status was required. At stake was the continuity of the paternal seed, which for centuries had served as reference in the continuity and preservation of the family and the nation and, metaphorically speaking, of the species itself. Redemption of this continuity lay no longer within the natural order, the body, and procreation, but within the sphere of a symbolic understanding that disobeyed what had been "right" in the past, breaking with this right and proposing a new, "treasonous" way of perceiving reality.

Here was the repetition of a discovery made as far back as Adam and Eve: preservation of the species depends upon both obedience and disobedience to the status quo, that is, on disobedience to the animal morality reigning at any given moment. Adam and Eve's morality, which prohibited them to eat of the Tree, had to be breached to permit the true continuity of the human species.

SALVATION THROUGH BETRAYAL: THE MESSIANIC LINEAGE

One of the most intriguing questions in biblical genealogy concerns the Messiah's family roots. Traditionally identified as a descendant of the House of David, the Messiah is heir to a fascinating lineage, marked by profound transgressions, as observed by the anthropologist Claude Lévi-Strauss.[16] Let us take a brief look at this genealogy.

The Book of Genesis tells the story of the destruction of two wicked cities, Sodom and Gomorrah. Wracked by major convulsions in the realm of "right" and "good" in the eyes of the Eternal One, these societies met with catastrophic destruction. The only nuclear family to escape with their lives was Lot, his wife, and two daughters. But when Lot's wife turned around to see what was happening and watch how the cities were being destroyed, she was turned into a pillar of salt. In terror, Lot and his two daughters hid in a cave. Believing the whole world had been destroyed, the older daughter said to the younger one: "Our father is growing old, and there is no other man left in the world to marry us in a normal manner. Come, let's get our father drunk with wine, and sleep with him, and we will survive through children of our father." The text goes on to say: "That night, they got their father drunk with wine, and the older girl went and slept with her father. He was not aware that she had lain down or gotten up. The next day, the older girl said to the younger, 'Last night it was I who slept with my father. Tonight, let's get him drunk with wine again. You go sleep with him, and we will survive through children of our father.' Lot's two daughters became pregnant from their father. The older girl had a son, and she named him Moab. He is the ancestor of [the nation] Moab that exists today. The younger girl also had a son, and she named him Ben-Ami. He is the ancestor of the people of Ammon who exist today" (Genesis 19:31–38, Aryeh Kaplan translation).

Believing that the entire world had been destroyed, Lot's daughters felt responsible for the continuity of the species. In biblical terms, they were guaranteeing that their father's endangered seed would live on. The sons begotten of these relations carry this distinction in their names: Moab (whose name means "from the father") is a son of his father, and Ben-Ami, ("from my people") a son of the people. Lot's daughters ensured the survival not only of their father's seed but of the entire people's seed. Yet the solution they found—incest—transgresses biblical law. "Good"—in this case, survival of the species—is saved by a new "right," and this entails a betrayal of the law that is neither condemned nor judged by the biblical text. Thus began one of the lines of the House of David and, consequently, of the Messiah.

Later on, in chapter 38 of Genesis, we find a second lineage. This is the episode where Judah, son of Jacob, fails to obey the law of the levirate. According to this law, if a married man died without leaving children, his brother (or closest relative) had to take the widow as his wife and impregnate her to ensure continuity of the deceased's lineage. These "redeemers of the seed" played an important, respected role in biblical times.

Judah had three sons—Er, Onan, and Shelah—and he found a woman named Tamar to be his firstborn's wife. When Er died without leaving any descendants, Judah obliged Onan to fulfill his obligation as brother-in-law. But, the Bible tells us, since Onan knew that the offspring would not be his, he spilled his semen on the ground whenever he went to his brother's wife, so that he would not have children in his brother's name (Genesis 38:9). This is the origin of the term "onanism" (masturbation), derived from Onan's decision to deny his sperm to Tamar, wasting it instead.

Judah told his daughter-in-law Tamar to live as a widow in her father's house until Judah's son Shelah was grown, because he feared that Shelah would die too, like his brothers. A long time passed without any redeemer propagating the seed of Judah's sons through Tamar. Meanwhile, Judah's wife died, and Tamar heard that he was going to Timnah to shear his sheep. Tamar dressed as a prostitute and sat waiting for her father-in-law on the road, to proposition him. Since Judah had no way of paying Tamar on the spot, he left "pledges" with her (his signet, cord, and staff) as proof of his debt. Since the "prostitute" disappeared, Judah never got his belongings back.

Some months later, Judah was told his daughter-in-law was pregnant, and he demanded she be put to death for committing adultery. So Tamar showed him his belongings and Judah shamefully recognized she had acted correctly when she ransomed the seed that had been denied her. Tamar bore twins: Perez and Zerah.

Once again, the redemption, or preservation, of the seed transpired in irregular fashion. Tamar is not only dissimulating when she passes herself off as a prostitute (as when Lot's daughters got him drunk); the story likewise involves signs of incest, since Tamar redeems her husband's seed through her father-in-law rather than her brother-in-law. Transgression — once again committed by a woman — recaptures the possibility of propagation. The law is fulfilled through disobedience and betrayal.

Traced back to transgressions committed to preserve continuity, these two genealogical lines cross in the story of Ruth. Set in the countryside during harvest time, the story uses the word *seed* in two senses.

A member of the tribe of Judah called Elimelech migrated with his wife, Naomi, and their two sons to the land of Moab, fleeing a severe drought. There his sons married Moabite women, and Elimelech passed away. Not long afterward, his two sons died as well. Naomi released her two daughters-in-law of any responsibility toward her, insisting they rebuild their own lives since they were still young. But one of them, Ruth, refused to abandon her mother-in-law, because she knew that without Ruth, Naomi would never be able to redeem her husband's seed. With no living sons, it was as if Naomi made use of the law of the levirate to redeem her husband's lineage.

Full of details rich in symbolism, this story tells how Ruth managed to recover the potential for propagating the family. Like a beggar, Ruth went to glean "seeds" remaining in the field of Boaz, a rich relative of Elimelech. Boaz took an interest in

Ruth, even though he was of an older generation—the same as Elimelech, Ruth's father-in-law—and he offered her "seeds" so she would not die of hunger.

Naomi and Ruth grew excited over the possibility of redeeming their husbands' seeds. With Naomi's help, Ruth made plans to seduce Boaz. Amid the festivities to celebrate the end of harvesting, surrounded on all sides by seeds, Boaz got drunk, and Ruth went to lie at his feet. The Bible is unclear about whether or not Ruth got the desired "seed" from the rich farmer in order to continue her husband's lineage.

Boaz in any case ends up coming to Ruth's aid, taking her as his wife, and in the final chapter of Ruth, the reader discovers that Boaz was a descendant of Perez, Judah's son by his daughter-in-law Tamar. The Moabite Ruth was a descendant of Moab, the incestuous son of Lot by his eldest daughter. From the union of these two transgressive lines—through Boaz and Ruth—King David will be born. And from the House of David will come the Messiah—in truth, a descendant of "saviors and redeemers" of seeds through transgressive acts.

What we inarguably have here is a pattern initiated by Eve, who gets Adam involved; the eldest daughter, who gets Lot drunk; the daughter-in-law, who fools Judah; and Ruth, who seduces Boaz. In all of these cases, it is the woman who, through disobedience, constructs humanity's road and redeems not only its seed but its very future.

Lévi-Strauss points out this gradual cloaking of the incestuous act, which began quite explicitly with Lot and his daughters but almost disappears in the case of Boaz and Ruth. Transgression is disguised but it in fact guides the body's destiny.

The fundamental issue here appears to be the fact that natural processes, the law, and that which is deemed "right" fail to achieve the desired "good." It becomes necessary to create a new order, one that can be extremely immoral at a given moment but which will ensure continuity and preservation. If you are able to follow this road, you endow the soul with its due value while bringing about the demise of the body and its animal morality.

We find the same transgression within the family of Moses. Although he is not of messianic lineage, Moses will play the historical role of Israel's redeemer in the episode where the Hebrews flee Egypt. In a comment apparently of little importance to the accounting of events, Exodus 6:20 makes a point of telling us that Moses' father was Amram, who married his own aunt, Jochebed. The Bible prohibits such a marriage (Leviticus 18:12), deeming it incestuous. Moses' history reveals this same theme of the endangered seed. Pharaoh decrees the annihilation of the seed, yet it is preserved—not simply through the prohibited marriage of Moses' parents but, once again, through a woman's initiative in the act of redemption.

As in the stories of the Messiah's ancestors (Lot's daughters, Tamar, and Ruth), it will be up to women to decide the paths of this redemptive transgression. In this particular case, the women act together: midwives (who disobey the order to kill newborns), Moses' mother and sister (who redeem the seed, placing the baby Moses in a basket in the Nile), and Pharaoh's daughter as well (who completes the redemption by adopting the baby). It falls to the woman to redeem the seed, albeit using strategies that transgress the reigning morality in order to reach the final goal.

The Messiah's ancestors were traitors of the reigning morality and customs, and in the eyes of the establishment there is nothing more devilish or threatening than the interests of those who break with the status quo in order to assure the best possible chances for individual and collective survival. Seen from the perspective of preservation, the Messiah is represented within the collective human imagination as a subversive, a nihilist, and a heretic.

Ultimate Transgressions

During the Roman invasion, it is not hard to identify the signs that characterized possible saviors—candidates to redeem the seed of Israel. The individual would not only have to restore the Jewish people's autonomy but would above all have to be able to redeem the seedless father, or nation.

The switch from the patrilineal to the matrilineal model meant that the law allowed women who had been impregnated as a result of rape to seek a redeemer. At the level of popular myth, however, this only fulfilled a formality. A new concept would have to be created so that the propagation of Israel would be ensured. The issue was not that a father would have no off-spring but that there would be children with no father. Someone would have to assume the paternity of these children, who, un-like bastards, represented the hope of transforming a tragic situation into a miracle. It would fall to God—no one less than the Creator, the father of all—to assume this paternity.

Thus the Messiah's genealogy saw its continuity. Miriam (Mary)—just like Lot's daughters, Tamar, and Ruth—would likewise achieve this redemption of Israel's seed. Unlike her ancestors, Miriam was wholly protected from transgression, with the "virgin birth" covering a curious fact: Jesus' father is the Father of all. In other words, he was Mary's Father as well, and she bore a true descendant of Moab—of "my" father—as Lot's daughter had done when the Messiah's genealogical line began.

I hope it is quite clear that this is a historical perspective and does not imply any theological conclusion. What this interpretation actually does is reveal a commendable act of inversion by the Jewish people at the most humble levels of society, recognizing in the episode of national tragedy the beginning of their liberation. What appeared to represent the power of Roman conquest—by disgracing the wombs of the Jewish people—transformed itself into a great revolution through the use of betrayal and transgression as tools to neutralize a sordid side of our world. Just as, according to the prophetic image, swords will be turned to plowshares and spears into pruning hooks, so will the bastard produce the saint. When used in alliance with the human capacity to redesign "good," what is apparently "not right" allows a new right to emerge, transforming profane reality into sacred reality.

It is no mere coincidence that Jesus was born during Hanukkah, the Festival of Lights, during the winter solstice. The darkest night of the year produced the festival of hope, in which candles are lit in the midst of darkness. This light is not real but rather created from human hope. To a certain extent, it is a transgression of the natural state of night. Most important, it represents the possibility that out of darkness and the profane may come the light that will lead to spring and to the sacred as well. This subversion—already present in Jewish tradition through the idea of the rededication of the Temple during the time of the Maccabeans, when the House of God was recovered from the impurity of idolatry—is marked by the concept of "bastard power." What is impure can become purer than that which is by nature pure. The longest day of the year cannot produce the same hope that the longest night can produce. This is the perspective of bastard power that we find in Hebrew culture: the smallest, the weakest, the one who has experienced the hardships of life and of injustice—here we truly have the superman.

During the twentieth century, when a Jew (Jerry Siegel) created the comic-book character Superman, he rendered a symbolic interpretation of his world, heavily imbued with Jewish metaphor. Despite the destruction of the Jewish world—Europe/Krypton—he who will redeem the seed lives on in the new world. "The Other"—the son who is not a son—drops into the heart of a typical American family, but even so he will redeem the seed. This outsider, this redeemer of his species, is to outward appearances the meek Clark Kent, while inwardly he inhabits a superhuman world, as a mutant. The survivor is the mutant who made himself different and more powerful, for to survive he had to save his body but above all he was forced to revise notions of "right" and "good." In Krypton, Superman is an ordinary guy. But when he survives the crossing from one bank to another—from one planet to another—he discovers that he has special powers.

Darkness that becomes light thanks to human hope is symbolic of the power someone holds by virtue of being an outsider and not being prototypical of the "perfect body."

Psalm 146 outlines the notion that the divine power of the God of Israel emanates from His being the protector of strangers, widows, and the fatherless. In contrast with the expectation that strength and virility are the best ways of assuring propagation of the species, little by little the notion is sketched out that Israel's future will be produced by the meek—so long as these individuals are transgressors. A proper family or correct behavior does not produce the species' best individual, as does the orphan, the widow, the prostitute, the stranger, or the outsider.

Like the patriarch Abraham, he who is able to leave his "house" and culture—the stranger or the outsider—is the superman that the future will produce on a mass scale.

Even in the Jewish rabbinical tradition, the Messiah—often represented by the prophet Elijah ("he who announces his arrival")—disguises himself as an outsider. He is the beggar who outwardly commands no respect but who in essence, as a man with no attachments, is powerful. Like an orphan, a bastard is also a foreigner, and his chances of being the new "chosen one" are great—the true, transgressive redeemer of the seed.

The passion that produces a messianic model could not derive from a model family, exemplary of the finest animal morality. It could derive only from the ability to transcend that which is "right." But the historical source of this inversion is a model

81

family of national suffering and of the open wound of the "redemption of the seed of Israel."

None of the families of Israel's past were exemplary. The patriarchs and matriarchs displayed odd personality quirks, weaknesses, and limitations, all of which are part of the great drama of transforming the worldly into the sacred. This memory is untouchable, and the representation of these archetypes now seems holy—but only after a profound process of transgression against the reigning cultures and moralities. A reader who tries to understand these biblical lives in literal fashion will fail to grasp how such figures can come out immaculate and without transgressing expectations of perfection and, therefore, models of morality.

For Israel, faced with the threat of national destruction, the messianic symbol of redemption of the seed is pushed to the top of the agenda, for its destiny is to be "father of a multitude"—not a father solely by way of being fruitful and multiplying, but "father" of all who endeavor to transgress the protected Eden of morality and culture that each new generation reconstructs.

With each generation, a new "garden" is designed, a new territory where the human being's concern with reproduction finds its space. This morality appears to be the way to collectively obtain the best results in propagating the species. It falls to each generation to repeat the first family's act of disobedience and to perpetuate not only the human species but its nature as well: co-creator and the only species capable of understanding not simply divine commandments but divine prohibitions as well.

Judging Body and Soul

A difficult truth that must be reestablished is that Jesus spoke in the language of Judaism. At no point do either his values or his discourse deviate from what is to be found in Israel's past, whether we are speaking of its patriarchs and matriarchs, of the liberating symbols of the Exodus, of the prophets' demands and poetry, or even of the Jewish discourse of Jesus' time, as found in such treatises as the *Ethics of the Fathers* (*Pirkei Avot*). Representing an effort of the collective ethical heritage, the latter work is of interest to anyone wishing to discover the values and discourse of those days. In it, we find teachings that speak in favor of suspicion, the redefinition of power, detachment from material illusions, and devotion to study and personal growth. The basis of this work is to lend legitimacy to what formerly appeared to be the greatest transgression: fulfillment of the destiny of eating from the Tree of Knowledge.

When Jesus accuses the sacerdotal leadership of being in collusion with Roman power, selling the "seed" of Israel for personal profit, this is the discourse of his people. As representative of this voice and in the condition of outsider, the historical Jesus is assigned the role of redeemer of Israel's true cause. As redeemer of the seed, he also sets before Israel proposals to take a road out of the land of conformity in search of new "rights."

The climate of political scheming reveals the interests of Rome and of the privileged citizens of Israel, who did not question Roman power—in contraposition to the majority of the people of Israel, who understood that the "seed" was in danger and who urgently needed a redeemer. Roman power was opposed to the Jews, which is rather a different reality than the one portrayed by the early Christian Church. The Church saw Jesus as representing a new Jew who stood in juxtaposition to the "old Jew," while Rome was the neutral power that washed its hands.

One of the most intriguing accounts in the Gospels is the story of the people's judgment of Jesus at the same time that the thief Barabbas is on trial. This accounting has profound consequences since it sets the ground for laying blame on the Jews for

Jesus' execution, insofar as they chose to free a criminal and condemn a saint. Who was in fact being condemned? Was it he who deviated from right without proposing a new good (Barabbas), or he who deviated from right and proposed a new good (Jesus)? Symbolically, this is what was being decided.

Let us examine one very interesting detail. The name Barabbas—or Bar ha-Aba in the original Aramaic—translates literally as "son of the father." According to Jewish tradition, individuals had no last names but were called "So-and-So, son (or daughter) of So-and-So." Individuals who had no defined paternity could call themselves "son of the father," interpretable either symbolically (divine paternity) or even ironically. Found at the center of the messianic tension of the redemption of fatherless children, which jeopardized the propagation of the Jewish people, this designation is most significant. Numerous modern works—including the polemic film on the life of Jesus entitled *The Last Temptation of Christ*—offer a range of possible interpretations of this trial. One of these interpretations, found in this movie, is that Jesus was not condemned and that there were not two men on trial but only one: Jesus, the *bar ha-aba*, son of the father.

Another symbolic possibility is that this was a trial of right and of good. Which would win out: "right," which is the true biological origin of he who carries the stigma of being the "fatherless child," or "good," which understands Jesus to represent true transformation by means of transgression, thus imposing a new good? In other words, what was on trial: the body, which denotes the true origin of the seed, or the soul, which is the ability to reinterpret reality through the prism of transgression? On the one hand lies morality, which sees the "son of a father" as a bastard; on the other, the immorality of the "son of the Father," who is superhuman.

The verdict is handed down by the establishment, and for the establishment there is no doubt: crucify transgression, for it jeopardizes animal morality; it exposes the nakedness that embarrasses us all. It sullies the true meaning of family and endangers property and tradition. The Jews were not part of the establishment; they were the vanquished, the oppressed, and the subjugated, and for this reason it is wrong to think their interests were represented here. Rome symbolizes the establishment, but through the filters and designs of history, it emerges as a mere spectator of events.

Companions to the historical Jesus in their resistance to the establishment, the thousands of Jews martyred during this period evince this reality. Many of those who were arrested with Jesus during celebration of the Jewish Passover dreamed of reestablishing the transgressive freedom of the past, when the people dared cross the sea, overcoming the inertia of pitched camps and alienation. The establishment represented by Rome and by its collaborators had no doubts about whom to condemn. The immoral soul had to be severely punished for checkmating the body's logic.

The Betrayer Betrayed

Quests of the soul are very frightening. They allow us to glimpse a potential new "good" without necessarily showing us the new "right" that will accompany it. The absence of this new "right" is deeply threatening to the human being, and at a subconscious level. The stances taken by the soul seem to threaten the very survival of the body, and our commitments to our body are inalienable. The commandment to preserve our species, or body, is powerful enough to make us doubt the rightness of our transgressions or make us resist their temptation.

Jesus is betrayed because he is the protagonist of a passion, who reveals himself as a traitor of accepted customs and morality. His radical stances in defense of the soul's causes raised fears that instead of redeeming the seed he would end up exposing it to great risks, decreasing the chances for re-demption. The positive commandment to procreate and to preserve is capable of generating violent reactions against the rebellious proposal to redefine "right."

Jesus' great betrayal was not, however, perpetrated against the Jews. After all, being a martyr in a conquered nation under great pressure from the conquerors is no rare thing. It is not surprising that such an incisive challenge to the ruling powers would generate a reaction as violent as crucifixion. Rome did not betray Jesus—it sacrificed him because it had recognized in him a dangerous enemy from the very beginning. The Jews did not betray him, because for one single reason they shared with him a sorrowful fate: just like the good citizen Jesus, a product of his culture, and bearing in mind the recognized value of transgression down through their history, the Jews continued to challenge constituted powers and to accept nothing but the ul-timate sovereignty of their God. The Jews' refusal to be subju-gated, their obstinate struggle to establish a new "good," and their faith that the necessary "rights" would naturally emerge had characterized the path of the Jews and their exile.

The early Roman Catholic Church, however, espoused an-other symbolic interpretation. Jesus came to be represented as the organizer of the ideal family, the greatest symbol of prop-erty and tradition, guardian of universal morality. It obliterated the transgression that transformed the son of a father into son of the Father and embraced a morality that policed behavior, which could in no way deviate from the norm. Little by little, the Church became guardian of the body and enemy of the soul's temptations. The concept of "original sin" was instituted to describe Adam and Eve's transgression, and their behavior was deemed reprehensible.

Anyone who had anything different to say about betrayal was condemned, while the Jew—a category that applied to the historical Jesus, ideologically and symbolically—was transformed into a traitor. The Jew was fashioned into the driving force behind the interests of the body rather than of the soul, an individual who sought the rigidity of laws at the expense of the transgressive flexibility of compassion. The body was interpreted as generating temptations and transgressions, while the soul became the stronghold of purity and the human being's immutable essence.

The perfect family no longer included the transgressor reintegrated into the category of "right" but was seen as "right" itself. The model family should consist of women dedicated to religion—that is, nuns devoted to Jesus, reproducing Mary's behavior—or of celibate priests, who reproduced the figure of Jesus. The body, now transgressive, threatened the purity of the soul, which was responsible for creating a suitable world that would lead to the fulfillment of the human being's greater interests. Good behavior, dogmas, and hierarchy were the soul's weapons in exorcising the body's diabolical transgressions.

Language changed, and interests that had previously been seen as represented by the body—the attitudes that sought to preserve the species through reliance on a morality that guaranteed the best conditions for doing so—were now seen as interests of the soul. "Saving the souls" of nonbelievers was the new language for "redeeming the seed." The language of the body, represented by the effort to safeguard its seed, was abandoned and a new one adopted in its place, thus subverting what had been the most central of human duties. Jesus had represented the interests of outsiders—the orphan, the ill, the prostitute—including his defenseless people, who obstinately sought their freedom and had challenged the establishment. Yet he was deemed a representative of the very segments of society with which he had entered into conflict at the cost of his life.

Jesus was killed by the interests of the body, which opposed his stances favoring the interests of the soul. The soul, now disguised as the body, condemns the body, which hides the soul. Upon the scaffold erected to execute not just the body but also its diabolical struggles to keep humanity from attaining a new "good," a cry of surprise goes up from the crowd when the criminal's hood is removed. It is not the body that has been executed, but the soul. The crucifixion would be perpetrated by the interests of morality and of the establishment.

The Saga of Judas: The Jew

The events that transpired during the first century of the common era saw the Roman Church and Judaism following two different paths of reorganization. While the Church established itself as part of the Roman Empire and organized itself around the structure of the past, re-creating its own version of the Temple and its sacerdotal hierarchy, Judaism underwent a profound revolution. With the destruction of the Temple in the year 70, the rabbis radically altered their practices and structure. In point of fact, both Christianity and Judaism abandoned the "right" of the past and established a new practice, or new "right," represented by the "house of assembly"—the church or synagogue—instead of the Temple, and by rituals that used words (prayer) instead of sacrifices. The new "good"—the "good news"—would, however, take a different direction in the case of the descendants of Israel.

The rabbis—a group to which Jesus quite likely belonged—offered the people a leadership concerned with safeguarding Israel's "transgressive" essence. The group comprised "masters" (the meaning of the word *rabbi*) who had other occupations: shoemakers, carpenters, fishermen. These men did away with Judaism's sacerdotal leadership, resulting in a profound democratization of authority. They were returning to the biblical definition itself, which described the Hebrews as "a nation of priests" (Exodus 19:6).

The rabbis enjoyed no special privileges or rights, and this is still true today. Any Jew may perform a marriage, a burial, or a blessing, with no need for an authority to be present. These rabbis also initiated the compilation of the Mishnah and the Talmud, which would become forums of national debate in exile, wherein the oral law was forged by gathering the opinions of the sages and allowing controversies to enrich and refine issues. There was no longer any central hierarchy but rather an authority administrated by masters whose legitimacy was based on their knowledge and wisdom rather than on a title or appointment. The minority opinion was recorded along with the majority opinion, so that "right"—that is, the law—could at any moment in history be reviewed and revised. The rabbis radically embraced the interpretative method that reads texts from nonliteral angles. It is this same method that permits the transgression of deeming what is immoral or not right as the new moral or new right.

A short tale from the Talmud (*Baba Metziah*) illustrates rabbinical aversion to any authority that claims itself as a representative of divine will and dogma. It is told that Rabbi Eleazar disagreed with the other rabbis and wanted to prove to them that he was right to evoke paranormal situations. So Rabbi Eleazar proclaimed: "If I am right, may this river change the course of its waters." And so it happened. The rabbis were not convinced. Rabbi Eleazar roared out: "If I am right, may this tree move from its place." And the tree shifted place some fifty meters. But the rabbis still weren't convinced. Finally, Rabbi Eleazar convoked the divine presence: "If I am right, may a voice from heaven come and declare it so." And a heavenly voice was heard to say: "The law lies with Rabbi Eleazar." The other rabbis immediately reacted by quoting part of a verse that says: "The Torah lies not in the heavens." The right of interpretation and the human effort to find its own paths do not require interventions in the name of the Truth.

The rabbis chose a path of great democratic, humanist tenor, where the stranger, the defenseless, and the outsider enjoy a position of respect. This option was a continuation of the biblical and prophetic ideals that inspired the life and activism of the historical Jesus.

The Church, on the other hand, structured itself much as in the past. It created a center, or Temple, in Vatican City, and reorganized itself as a sacerdotal caste with corporatist interests, as had transpired at the Temple in Jerusalem. A "great priest" was elected, and only a select group continued to wear a skullcap. Holy rites could be performed only by priests, who acted as intermediaries between the people and God. The Church aligned itself with the interests of kingdoms, feuds, and the nobility in general and began to condemn those who thought differently, eliminating the possibility of salvation for those who did not follow its guidelines and sentencing a substantial number of individuals to martyrdom. Sacrificed because of their ideas, these individuals were treated as heretics and traitors to a cause that certainly had not been Jesus'; for Jesus himself would not have survived either the doctrinaire demands of the Church or its sinister political alliances aimed at earthly power that so distanced the Church from the common folk and marginal people.

For over a millennium, from the Middle Ages up to modern times, the Church acted as a self-proclaimed ideological and theological watchdog, imposing its law through its executive branches, including the Inquisition. The burned witches and Judaizers were prostitutes, protestors, visionaries. They were not just the people or group with whom Jesus was identified — symbolically, they *were* Jesus.

It was only in this century, following persecution in the form of pogroms and the Holocaust, that Jews began almost unconsciously to portray themselves as crucified. In such paintings as *The Martyr* (1940) and *The Crucified* (1944), Marc Chagall (1887–1985) left a registry of the subconscious intersection of traitor and betrayed. Not that the persecutions were produced by the Church, but this institution's age-old view of the Jew as traitor left Europe ripe for the ultimate act of liberation from the transgressive threat that haunts the fantasies of all societies and all generations.

The cross, a meeting of vertical and horizontal, represents the plane of the body or earth (horizontal) and the plane of the soul or the heavens (vertical). Jesus dies because it is hard for us to remain loyal enough on both planes. Humanity, along with Jesus as symbol, is firmly rooted both in the devotion with which we ensure the multiplication and preservation of the species and in the profound need for transcendence and therefore for transgression (the vertical plane). When the horizontal segment (interests of the body) is overemphasized—as was the case of the corrupted Temple of Jerusalem or the medieval Catholic Church—the vertical segment of the soul will react violently.

Judas was not so much a Jew as Jesus was, and no institution has made this clearer than the Roman Catholic Church itself. The historical Jesus is no worshiper of what is right, or of the family, property, and tradition: his dangerous origin transgressed cultures and morals, and even today he would be sacrificed. The first to crucify him would be those who could not stand his compassion and his complaisance toward deviants, delinquents, and outsiders. It would not be farfetched to say that in certain traditional circles of Christian devotion, the historical figure would still be imprisoned and crucified.

As the traitor into which he was transformed, the Jew lurks about haunting everyone. He is both the one who crucifies—the establishment—and the one who is crucified—the nonconformist. He is the son-of-a-father thief judged alongside the son-of-the-Father saint. The latter is the one who is sacrificed, while the former is freed to be the stigma of generations. The son of a father, the unredeemed seed—this is the Jew the Church wanted to construct. Rather than make the effort to turn a deviant into a holy man, it presented him as a bastard mutant.

PRODUCT OF THE SOUL: A MUTANT

Among the fears that plague the collective subconscious, the fear of failing to redeem the seed occupies a special place. From the time of the patriarchs and matriarchs, the issue of primogeniture and of which son is best fit to redeem the seed was a complex one. For the sake of this redemption, transgressions were a constant, for the law of primogeniture did not always admit the best solution. Within the archetypal realm of the first families, Abraham transgresses when he tries to redeem his seed, passing over Ishmael to the benefit of Isaac; this is what Isaac does when he redeems Jacob, passing over Esau; this is what Jacob does with Joseph, passing over Reuben. There is, however, a difference between the transgressions of the patriarchs and matriarchs and those committed within the messianic lineage.

In the first case, the transgressions involved children of definite paternity. It was a question of deciding who was the fittest. In the messianic case, the transgressions meant selecting the fittest not as determined by personality traits but as determined by social conditions. The poor, the destitute, the stranger, and the outsider are better prepared to pick up camp and follow the paths of evolution than the well adapted, who always find ways of transforming their desire to remain in a narrow space into ideology, morals, and theology. Temporarily strengthened, these individuals do not perceive the twists and turns of reality that will render their survival infeasible with the passing of generations. Those who have not become part of the establishment or have not conformed maintain more honest bonds with life's dynamics, leaning more toward detachment than control. From the perspective of the soul, the poor person is more fit for survival than the rich person; the bastard, more than the spoiled child; the afflicted, more than the fortunate; or the one from afar, more than the one nearby.

In some way, the messianic line came to represent the tension between body and soul found in what has become Western culture. It is not enough to defend continuity down through the fittest child—often breaching the law within the realm of the family. Those individuals among the species' collective offspring who are most fit to ensure continuity of the social and historical process should be empowered, so that a new human being can be created and, as transgressor of the body's limitations, increase the species' chances of survival.

Breaching this collective law of choosing the fittest individual constitutes a betrayal of the social perception that this individual is indeed the fittest and most well adapted to the reigning set of morals. Society's "firstborn," the "goody-goody" who is a perfect example of these morals, is here to be usurped and betrayed. This betrayal is one of the species' hidden desires yet deeply threatens everyone's quality of life. For today's traitor himself will establish new norms that will in turn make him fear being betrayed. In both individual and collective terms, let there be no doubt: the greatest enemy lies within ourselves. It is the subversive who may spoil the party by showing us that our space has grown too narrow.

People who find the soul's transgressions anxiety-provoking often ask, "When you have much more than you need, why risk it?" People are bothered when someone starts violating concepts and norms of the past, because their identification with this process sparks fear and discomfort. Aware that the greatest threat to their own current interests lies within themselves, they still recognize that they cannot renounce their future. Detachment fuels much conflict within human beings, equipped as we are with the ability to obey and to disobey.

Biblical metaphor presents the human being as the animal

that can be guided by its instincts but also by its power to choose (which is not always compatible with its instincts). Thus was produced the fittest and most insecure of all the species. The human body attacks to defend its territory but also crucifies to defend itself from its own soul. In the past, its predators were both external and internal. Today, the internal ones are the most deadly.

Strange as it may seem, this naked, conscious animal began experiencing a new dimension of its environment and the relationships involved in its survival. Its instinct and senses were no longer focused solely on the outer world but also on the inner. The noises and movements that put the human being in a state of alert were not produced only by other human beings around him but also by a soul that dwelled within him.

The wondrous beauty of the "passion" that conquered the West is found not solely in tradition but in betrayal. Of the multitude of betrayals described in this book, the one that stands out most is the act of treason that divinizes someone who has condemned himself to sacrifice. The subconscious device of consecrating the "criminal" and damning the "saint" derives from the great ambivalence produced by the human being's greatest tool for survival, which is likewise our greatest threat. Morality and immorality will be everlasting companions for as long as the human species endeavors to survive. Its God commands and retracts His commandment. The human hero will be acclaimed and then immediately brought to sacrifice. The finest human reproduction will not be the Aryan but the bastard—not the clone but the mutant.

THE MESSIAH: SAVIOR OR CRIMINAL?

It is not surprising that the notion of Messiah traces its roots to Judaism. The challenge of Abraham's descendants was to teach the generations to come the ability and courage to leave their own house, legitimizing the "sin" of Adam and Eve, who left their Garden. Abraham would be the first to propose a positive image of Adam and Eve's betrayal by veiling the transgressive aspect of their behavior and inaugurating a new concept of God, one cast not merely in terms of disobedience but as a God who declares and then retracts a declaration. This is a one and only God, because in order to adopt two different ideas, what is necessary is not two gods but rather the human ability to legitimate evolution, translating it into culture and morals. In point of fact, this Abrahamic morality became quite confused with the "immorality" of which his descendants were accused and for which they were victimized during medieval times and in early-twentieth-century Europe. The roots of anti-Semitism—a sentiment expressed even by Jews themselves—are grounded in this view of Abraham's descendants as a treacherous people who endanger any status quo.

As the Christian world's representative of this status quo, the Roman Catholic Church saw the image of the dangerous, threatening Jew in the prototypical figure of the historical Jesus. The "Jewish problem"—that is, the Jew's transgressive potential—became particularly unbearable for Europe during this century. Openly showing its "claws," Judaism left the medieval ghetto that had managed to isolate this "cancer" on society, and the ensuing metastases were identified in the academic world, the sciences, free trade, and left-wing social movements. Wherever Europe's dominating, colonizing world turned, it saw the shadow of the Jew who wanted to "conquer" the world. The Jews would dominate it through transgression, modifying it and threatening the interests of morality. The Jew's double loyalty—represented by his transgression of the modern concept of national loyalty—became the newest way of identifying him as society's parasite. Jews were accused of corroding society from the inside, like cancer, eroding its structures and perverting society's very cells. They were an all-out threat to survival. Only by surgically removing them would the world be assured of the needed cure. Thus, the perfect world, of the perfect Aryan child, would do away with those who represented the memory of the bastard child—and, what was worse, those who had once been diabolically capable of seeing this bastard as the "redeemer of the seed."

In their experiences of exile and crucifixion, the Jews had become the model of the survivor and of survival itself. Unsuccessful in the world of the body and of history, the Jews were champions of the soul, of adaptation through mobility, and of the ability to tolerate change. As people who came from "afar," the Jews acquired the blessing/damning label of "chosen ones" much more through external identification than through merit alone. A process natural to the human species had occurred: the more someone is a traitor and the more he or she is oppressed for being a traitor, the greater the admiration he or she wins as a "chosen person." The more the Jews were treated as traitors, the greater the effort to legitimate them as descendants of Abraham's tradition and the messianic tradition—for in point of fact, both traditions constitute treasons, and so their followers can only be traitors.

Nazism—one of history's greatest expressions of the effort to defend the moral body—dreamed of leading a revolution of the body that would give birth to a kingdom where immutability would reign for one thousand years. Orchestrating the forces of morality and of perfect children devoid of deformities, Nazism secretly proposed to eradicate the greatest evil. It was essential to wipe out the Roman myth of a Jesus betrayed by Jews, a myth that disguised the soul's transgressive element. Punishing the Jews, forcing them to convert, or making them into the big-nosed villains who make pacts with the devil would not do away with the monster but would only strengthen it. The solution was total eradication. Muddying the waters of history had backfired, and Jewish "wickedness" had gained strength down through the centuries, especially in Europe. For Hitler, the Jews were a threat that came from the right and from the left, from capitalism and from communism; his was a paranoia resembling the feeling of being persecuted by one's own shadow. Jewish bankers, Jewish dominance of the world of finance, and Jewish militancy in communist organizations were all demonstrations that the good traitor will betray either side.

At the same time, the Jewish merit of bringing "light unto the nations" was much more a product of the Jewish model than a choice born of the Jewish essence. The Jew had become a survivor, and as such he had learned to make good use of the tensions between body and soul. Above all, as required of a human survivor, he had relied on the soul's potential. This is what made him a banker or a Bolshevik, in both cases embracing an extreme. His ability to produce wealth and his radical social militancy derived from the legacy of obeying and disobeying. His relationship to risk proved truly efficacious. Though castigated by the shame produced by the body's morality, his model proved the efficiency of the "obedience/disobedience" model that created a survivor. The seed would be redeemed through this new man, a survivor.

The new man that the West saw personified in Jesus represents the centuries-old Jewish dream of a messianic era peopled by these new human beings. It will be a world of traitors who will not be sacrificed, a world that will understand that it is not others who do the crucifying but ourselves . . . a world where Jews will not be the Other, but ourselves. This will happen not because the Jews are the chosen people but because the Western world will decide to choose this symbol as a model for its redemptive transgression.

Understanding this does not mean consecrating the Jew or Judaism as superior. Rather, it reveals the symbolic structures that sustained the construction of Christian tradition. In many ways, the new discourse and the new covenant of Christianity, aimed at producing a new Israel, instead of replacing Judaism had symbolically empowered it. By attacking the Jews as representing the Other—the part of ourselves that makes us afraid—Christianity has bound Judaism to its own destiny.

The meaning of the name Israel as explained in the Bible— one who struggles with God—is simultaneously the greatest heresy and the holiest affirmation. On the one hand, it expresses disobedience and conflict; on the other, it voices a profound desire to encounter this God of many discourses, which allow creature and Creator to acquire a common language. In the eyes of God, right and good are constructed out of the now obsolete right and good that went before. The death of a god is the pathway toward God; it is the abandonment of one body to move toward another. Every body has a god, but only the tension between soul and body really brings us closer to God. Redeeming the seed means understanding that preservation of the species depends fundamentally on our transgressions, for this is the only way we will be parents of a "multitude" in another, conquered land, which is not the land of our obedience. This is the only way we will find peace in the consciousness of our finitude, because human beings find this peace by fulfilling designs and also by betraying them. If you seek only to obey, you will suffer the despair of no longer being in a protected garden— where animal peace was found through obedience to designs. In the world outside of paradise, relating to a savior whom we confuse with our executioner is part of reality.

We will still commit many crucifixions, but the ultimate one, the one that is truly at stake, is our own. If we fail to fashion some form of peace out of the tension between our body and our soul, between our animal morality and our spiritual immorality, we are in danger of failing to redeem our species. The Messiah in whom we place so much hope and whom we systematically crucify is alive within us, awaiting the peaceful companionship of the two antagonists that struggle within us. The relationship between tradition and treason plays a fundamental role in this endeavor.

The greatest companion of someone who is betrayed is his or her traitor, and vice versa. No one holds as many secrets about life and about well-being as these two partners. The desire to annihilate this Other is an act of suicide, for one thing is certain: betrayal is the gauge that warns us about the loss of a tension fundamental to the survival of our species. Wiping out the traitor means annihilating the betrayed; it means depriving the one who has been betrayed of the chance to perceive that wickedness may lie as much in obedience as in disobedience.

4 The Future of Betrayal

The question of survival emerges in Jewish tradition and then spreads through Christian tradition in the form of constant conflict. On the one hand, it makes fidelity to our animal condition an imperative, for the seed must be redeemed—and this fidelity is best preserved by creating optimum conditions for procreation. It requires recognition of the anatomic reality of sex, with its advantages and disadvantages. Little by little, this is what has organized society, reflecting the adaptive solutions civilization has found necessary over the course of time. Morality and many of our ethical concepts were designed to maximize our chances of preserving the species.

Issues like the environment continue to bear witness to the intense effort to reformulate our understanding of an individual's responsibilities and rights within a society whose overriding objective is self-preservation. This concern with redeeming the seed is found in the story of Noah's ark, which is a metaphor of humanity's own history. Depositing our seeds in an ark of time is the primordial commandment planted deep within our being. Paradoxically, the ark—plunged into the insecurity of hazardous waters, with no land in sight, threatened on all sides—is a comforting place filled with hope. This ark is the morality constructed by civilization. Sailing in search of a safe harbor, it represents the body's dream of disembarking in a new world, different from the one it left behind. That former world was so filled with constant threats, with such violence, that the anxiety of those who wished to be mothers and fathers bred hope of a better place. The Creator, father of all seeds, would fashion the conditions needed for this ideal world to become a reality.

The moment when the ark finds this harbor atop Mount Ararat inaugurates a phase in the human history of constructing law and morality. Noah's seven fundamental laws* stand as a monument to the investment in building a better society down through the subsequent years of human history. Rather than killing ourselves to accomplish the greatest role of our existence, we have established rules that endeavor to take into account the interests of everyone or of the majority, making it possible to achieve a strange dream—peace.

The question of the seed takes priority in the lives of Abraham and Sarah, of Isaac and Rebecca, of Jacob, Rachel, and Leah. Throughout the Bible, redemption of this seed is the driving force of the future, which fuels the dramas lived out by Lot and his daughters, by Judah and Tamar, by Boaz and Ruth, and by Miriam (Mary) and her redeemer. "Survival" became a

---

*In addition to the many commandments given to Jews in the Torah, there are seven basic commandments that were given to non-Jews at the time of Noah: do not deny God; do not blaspheme; do not murder; do not commit sexual offenses; do not steal; do not eat the limb of a living animal; and set up courts to ensure obedience to the other six laws.

revered word for the children of Israel, for they had created a tradition—the collective consciousness of their greatest obligation: procreation. The messianic dream meant reproducing the hope for a new Noah to continue navigating through history, leading us—that is, our seed—to a new world. This world would be morality's and the law's greatest conquest, establishing here on earth a celestial kingdom of guaranteed reproduction and, therefore, of profound peace.

On the other hand, another fidelity was imperative. The construction of morality and the law constrains and obstructs the process of consciousness, which in final analysis is the human being's most valuable tool for survival. Building culture means knowing how to destroy it in due time. Constructing morality means knowing how to breach it and leave your parents' house—parents who will devour the future unless you can break with the past, just as this past has been forged from the glory of many such prior ruptures. Tradition is the essential root that lends itself to be cut and betrayed. This new act of treason is the sap that will reconstitute an even stronger root.

Abraham wants to be father of a multitude, and for this reason he must hear what God has to tell him. But he truly becomes this father of a multitude when he is able to hear this God say something different from what he had said before. Evolution of the species lies in the silence of the father who raises the knife but then detains it; it lies in the silence that each man and each woman knows in their personal and collective lives—a challenging silence that responds to an impulse to disobey. This sacred disobedience is the element that human beings dream of integrating into their notion of peace. For most of our civilization, peace is a product of security and certainty. But deep down we all know that peace cannot be achieved by establishing an ideal world in which we all enjoy an immutable body. The dynamics of our being, which lives in a state of transformation, impelled creation of the concept of

soul, and the apparent conflict between our nature's two legitimate interests became expressed in the concepts of tradition
and betrayal.

Jesus' passion speaks of the sacrifice of the illegitimate child,
the sacrifice of "right" on behalf of "good." However, it is this
very child, in its illegitimate status, that has been constantly consecrated throughout Israel's history. The knife—weapon of the
crime—is left in Abraham's hand, as the body conspires against
the soul, whose only demand is the redemption of the legitimate son, the son of morality. In the symbolic realm, this moment initiated a conflict responsible for much violence and
many sacrifices. Far from the expected peace, what rose to the
surface was conflict.

As in psychological processes, exposing this intense conflict
that reflects the human need for tradition and betrayal could
prove of great therapeutic benefit. However, when the issues at
stake have such major impact on our perception of the world,
information does not lead to cognition. Traditions have often
become so powerful for this precise reason: we hear what we
want to and we perceive things in such a way that the world fits
into our existing vision of reality.

Projecting ourselves onto the Other and engaging in antag-
onisms serve the interests of the body, which uses any opportunity it can to isolate the soul lying inside the Other and thus
control it. But this "solution" to the problem is a false one.

Transcendence is not gained by controlling the body. The
body's purposes are here to be obeyed, and the body that wants
to control the body itself becomes inhuman. It is the soul, in its
condition of traitor, that is the great liberator, freeing the body
from oppression; for this reason the body has a fundamental
dependence on the soul. Redemption of the seed—or salvation—is not accomplished by covering our nakedness with
clothes. The garments that clothe human intentions in morality make us prisoners of a reality that clips our wings, constrains

us, and threatens our survival. Being able to see our nakedness, however, is a betrayal of our conscious animal, one that is hard to commit. Many of those who were burned at the stake before all the world wanted to expose this nudity.

Historically, in the West, Roman Catholicism has arrogated itself defender of true tradition and has named the Jew as the true traitor. The defense of the seed from the perspective of the body, which has included the canonization of the pure, immaculate family, is visible today in the Church's stances against abortion and birth control as unacceptable threats against the body's greatest commandment: be fruitful and multiply. The Jew is the corrupter who jeopardizes this exemplary family. His wickedness proposes that the world "leave the house" of its parents, which is precisely the family that has been built to best guarantee preservation. The proposal of leaving the family is identified with everything that threatens this family: abortion, sex outside of marriage, adultery, homosexuality, and depravity. The Jew's very existence demonstrates that the soul occupies a unique place within this construction of the body and that it conspires against this entire worldview.

Reluctant to embrace this conventional and conformist conception of the family, the Jew is in fact the inventor of the original transgression of transforming the illegitimate child into the most legitimate child. Although the Jew is unaware of this historical truth, the individual who has made himself the Jew's Other sees it clearly emblazoned on his forehead. And what truth might this be? The strength of tradition is created in this reversal, in the profound betrayal that identifies the son of the Father in the son of a father. Tradition has been forged through betrayal. As Lévi-Strauss has pointed out in regard to messianic descent, concealing the transgressive aspect that redeems both the seed and the future became an absolute issue for medieval Catholicism. This was made possible by "choosing" an Other who would serve to exorcise the treasonous element from tradition.

During the twentieth century, this behavior spread beyond the borders of any one tradition. Islamic as well as Jewish fundamentalism, evangelical groups, independent churches, and sects of all kinds have learned that a substantial part of the population finds it quite attractive to take the betrayal out of tradition. When these religions ritually exorcise the demon of "treason" and seek to redeem the purity of the family and of society, they commit a crucifixion and introduce a false messianic path. They undermine the sacred teaching of deep reverence for rupture with any authority lesser than the words of the God who commands and retracts Himself. The messianic world is not one that definitively establishes the celestial "right" here on earth. It is fashioned from a commitment to good, that is, to new "goods" that will re-create new "rights."

Jesus' purity is not genetic, and he is not the representative of "right." He symbolizes a possibility in which his tradition — the Jewish tradition — always believed: by transgressing against the violence of the past, a better world is reached. Preserving is as essential as modifying.

For Jewish tradition, the Messiah has not yet arrived. He will come not to sanction a definitive "right" but to sanction the profound peace that comes from living out tradition as well as treason. Humanity has not yet reached this stage. We continue to wander through history, terrified by one of our traits, the ability to betray.

Only when betrayal no longer injures the person betrayed or tradition itself — instead awakening both to the new possibilities unfolded by betrayal — will we witness the emergence of a world that goes beyond tolerance, a world of appreciation. The parents of the future will not see their child's leaving home as betrayal, but as an expansion of the home, which grows to contain a space no longer narrow. This ample new place will be as essential to survival as the question of the seed. In the future, the loved one who has been betrayed will be aware enough not to fall back on commitments or contracts made in the past. His or her pain will be mediated by a feeling of partnership in any betrayal committed by the Other. He or she will perceive the body's exercise of its morality as a natural movement that the soul will oppose.

This "ideal" world will nevertheless be filled with fears and misgivings, because these feelings are part of the nature of animals who obey and disobey. But in this new world there will be no crucifixions. The Other—the enemy and traitor—will not be the body or the soul but the loss of tension between both. The greatest enemy will be the perception that sees the Other as a source of danger. Such threats become much more real when we fail to use the two fantastic awarenesses planted in our human flesh: the awareness whose destiny it is to obey and the other, whose destiny it is to disobey.

THE INDIVIDUAL AND THE SOUL

In the Western world, the battle between tradition and betrayal receives special attention in the realm of the family. For the individual, the family represents tradition and is the organization that answers for reproductive interests and the interests of the body. The family is therefore the terrain of tradition and—as it would also have to be—of betrayal. Marriage is simply a contract, for it deals with an area where conflicts of interest occur. We generally believe that the conflicts in question stem from the differing interpretations that two individuals have. But conflict here derives much more from the tensions inherent to human nature than from differing viewpoints regarding rights and duties. The body introduced the institution of marriage, and it is precisely through the body that everyone betrays the institution. There is no way to avoid betraying a marriage if we do not recognize the tension lying within each individual, within each person's nature.

In his desire to fulfill his destiny to procreate, through his anatomy, man is always tempted by woman. When Eve first tempted man, it was not because of her sensuality, later to be repressed by tradition. It was because for man, she is the object through which he rediscovers that tension lies within him. Every time a man is tempted by a woman, he finds himself asking whether to preserve the "right" of the past or seek the "good" of the new moment. "Right" is just as important to his body as "good." From the viewpoint of the past, "right" preserves better; from the viewpoint of the future, "good" plays this role. The man who sublimates his passion or rebellion, putting up with a marriage that has become nothing more than tradition, is a betrayer. This marriage is sustained to assure survival of the seed, but it suffocates the feeling that redemption will truly come through betrayal. Its conception is grounded in a rigid "right," frightened by the shadows of the new "goods" that jeopardize both the contract and tradition. The man who breaches this contract by taking lovers also commits betrayal. He can commit a betrayal by preserving a marriage—that is, by maintaining the "old right" while using the "new good"—or by embracing a new contract. In the latter case, he is seeking a "new right" in order to achieve a "new good," but he will have to face the cruel awareness that this new right may itself, sometime in the future, become inappropriate as compared to another "good." This awareness weakens our desire to invest in the "new right," as we sense it to be as fragile as the "old right" in absolute terms. Most people succumb to one of these two approaches. Every man is a potential betrayer of his wife since it is possible that a new "good" will appear, affording better possibilities of fulfilling his destiny to procreate.

Woman is also a potential betrayer. Her urgent desire that Adam eat of the Tree reflects the dream that he taste as many trees as necessary to become more like God. Woman does not betray quantitatively, like man, but qualitatively. She waits for a prince or, conceived in perfect terms, for a marriage with God Himself. Male fantasies that women hold the power to devour them are built upon the female dream of an ideal man—a man who was expected to be the best possible "good" and who would justify the "right" signed under contract. But this expectation is frustrated when the woman realizes that the man is not ideal. Every time a woman sees a man who appears more willing to taste of the tree of transgression, of immortality, she is tempted to betray the "old right" for a "new good." The quality of this new "good" prompts the same temptation to betray that man feels. Men betray to redeem their seed outside the quantitative prison of monogamy; women betray to redeem their seed outside the qualitative prison of monogamy.

Betrayal will always be a choice for human beings who see themselves mythically as transgressors of paradise or as people who "leave their parents' house." This conflict may be resolved by recognizing its very existence and by establishing relations between men and women that admit these tensions as inherent to life itself. The ideal world of the future will be a world of tensions as well, but not of tensions projected onto the Other. The wish to exorcise the traitor inside ourselves by pointing at the Other is the nonmessianic circumstance of our civilization.

Much caution is required when living in a world where the Other, the deviant, is still crucified, yet where we cannot escape the responsibility of representing the interests of our mutant nature. Despite all dangers and risks, we must legitimate our body as well as our soul, for there is no other way to deal with our betrayals and find peace. These relations are vital to healing ourselves and are an indispensable tool in making our way through life.

The act of crucifixion takes place not only in the external world but also within each individual. A destructive potential lies at the point where horizontal and vertical meet, a potential for heavy guilt feelings that can paralyze and extinguish an individual's life and the chances for survival of the species. Knowing how to live at the point of this intersection without letting such legitimate and ambiguous impulses get the better of us is a secret that impacts our quality of life and allows us to better adapt and survive.

In the star of David, one triangle points up and the other points down. The one pointing downward indicates the sphere of obedience; the one pointing upward indicates the sacred sphere of disobedience. When Jacob flees after stealing his brother's birthright—fleeing in fact from himself—he dreams of angels going up and down a ladder. What Jacob wanted was to legitimate the angels' ascent and not their descent. He was endeavoring to justify the unbearable sense of holiness he felt in this upward climb, that is, in transgression. Marked by the quest to legitimate his act of disobedience against his "father"—his past and his God—Jacob's saga is an example of human tragedy and human glory.

Redemption of the truly human seed, which gives birth to tradition and treason, is the quintessential human question. Our days are consumed by this concern, for two worlds live within us: that of the betrayed and of the betrayer. Perhaps this is the imagery the Western world has produced: the Jew is all of us; all of us have Jewish blood in our veins. Thus we are the Other, the traitor.

Using the Other to speak of ourselves has had its wicked side, but above all it has revealed the intensity of the self-hatred that exists within human beings. Anti-Semitism is a sign of this self-hatred, as are wars and religious and ideological persecution. The deep pain triggered by recognition of this self-hatred involves an immediate acceptance of the fact that traitor and betrayed are one and the same person.

Any form of fidelity that does not encompass these two facets of human nature will provoke personal and collective crises. Our contemporary world currently faces a grave challenge. Camped beside a gigantic sea, the human species is confined to a world that has grown much narrower. It is narrow not only in its morality but in its rebellion: the repression of the Victorian era and the licentiousness of the hippie world both proved too narrow for human beings who little by little have realized that something different is needed. Alienation and the absence of "causes" are the clearest symptoms that this quest requires not the surgical removal of conflict but rather the effort to experience it fully within ourselves.

On the day the human being confronts his inner conflict, when he sees that his psychological integrity is threatened by two primordial desires, then the seas will part. When he crosses the ocean singing, impelled by his catharsis, he will find himself in the midst of another garden. There, everything will be prohibited and ready to be transgressed against. At peace with his soul, the human being will wander among various choices of disobedience. One tree, however, will not be prohibited. It will be the tree of the memory of a time when the notion of "right" served to veil fear and guilt. Walking hand in hand with the Creator, the immoral animal will have reencountered peace in his nakedness. Unclothed and aware of it, man will have found the long-awaited immortality of his soul. Forged out of immorality, this immortality will prove to be the Tree of Life. All trodden ground will be dry land amid the sea, and every body will be a bridge to a new body. Transgression will have been the human pathway through history toward transcendence—our long short path.

AFTERWORD

The Ultimate Scientific Discovery

We are on the verge of a fantastic discovery. The world is getting ready to witness one of science's greatest achievements: the Human Genome Project, the mapping of the human genes. This project has recognized some 300,000 genes that make up human DNA. For the first time, we are about to know the essence of the human body.

Genes are responsible for the information that determines our appearance (eye and hair color, height, and so on) as well as the condition of the internal organs that control bodily functions. Every single cell contains this original blueprint that determines whether a given cell will be in the kidney or in the heart, for example.

DNA's prime responsibility is reproduction. The order to be

fruitful and multiply is encoded in this intricate chemical tangle. In other words, the human being will know his body—the body he wishes to preserve. The human being now glimpses the opportunity to contribute toward the amazing preservation of life.

We cannot imagine what this knowledge may hold in store for the human body or for the corporeal part of life. Perhaps it will bring cures for diseases or ways of improving reproductive quality and efficacy. Individuals may be able to eliminate the tendency to develop a given disease right from birth. Sensations may be intensified or diminished, and many other wonders may become possible.

Yet the most incredible discovery will be the discovery of the soul. In the past, Newtonian physics conceived of a universe where time and space were exact, but this notion had to be rethought with the discovery of relativity. As our eyes saw the cosmos with greater precision and depth, and as mathematics grew more conceptual, reality proved itself to be more and more complex. The same is about to happen in the field of biology.

The Human Genome Project will gradually show us something that has already been hinted at in biological conjectures. I am referring to a curious phenomenon: when DNA is duplicated, a great number of errors occur. These design mistakes or "breakdowns" have been the cause of much discussion and speculation. How is it possible that a structure so perfect and so complex can tolerate what at first glance would appear to be glaring errors?

Any attempt to answer this question today would perhaps be as wise as trying to identify the shape of our planet before we had any notion at all that it was round. One piece of information, however, suggests that the process may be similar to how our understanding of relativity changed the field of physics. In designing coding material, nature does not always employ constant and error-free methods. To the contrary, we now know it allows for error and designs error recognition and repair mechanisms.

The Human Genome Project will not map the human being but rather *reveal* the human body. But as it will not totally account for the human being, it will propose the existence of another material, which is immaterial. Another kind of information is found in the cell, but it is free from obligation, free of the commandment to reproduce. Its concern is to challenge the body's status quo and to err. Its transgression dishonors the body and reproduces it differently than it was at first. This information is not chemical but is the backdrop for all chemistry. Materiality transgresses the very laws that it engendered.

By exclusion, the Human Genome Project will map the soul. It will be recognized in the form of a deviant chemistry, which reproduces errors and disobeys rules. We will then discover certain "discontinuities" in biology, which physics has already recognized in the cosmic universe. In recent decades, awed and surprised by their discoveries, physicists have dared to suggest that the concept of God is not illogical. Soon biologists will write books grounded on gaps in the human matrix of information and will move toward the notion of soul.

Biblical theory will then have proven a good approximation of how human nature is mapped. Its greatest commandment is to fulfill its role of preserving life and of multiplying. But the information that constitutes our beings would also appear to know what shouldn't be done, and it uses this awareness to obey or disobey. Deliberate error is the freedom of choice that allows us not only to fulfill orders and instructions but, if necessary, to disobey them.

Scientists are excited about the paths opening up before them, as they gradually become the heroes of redemption of the seed. The human dream of guaranteeing our seed is, however, only part of the task. Let them not forget that an establishment, or a scientistic tradition, will also be tormented by betrayals. These betrayals will be important, since the best so-lution for a society in a given era is not always the best form of self-preservation. Perhaps improper use of information in or-der to obey human desires for health and immediate preserva-tion will jeopardize future survival—a survival that depends upon errors, that is, upon the transgressions we may naively and presumptuously "correct."

The truth is we are just starting to crawl when it comes to our awareness of our task in this world. We will slowly come to understand that our mission is not only reproduction but delib-erate mutation—a mutation that requires us to be what we are not and that removes us from one body and takes us to another.

Like the field of science, I believe, we will know. As in the myth of the Tree of Knowledge, the genome and other great se-crets will be revealed to us. We will see our body in crystal-clear fashion. We will draw this body with even greater perfection than today's magnificent graphics, which show us precise skele-tons, organs, and circulatory systems. We will see the inner workings of matter and of corporeality. But, as in the myth, we will not reach immortality. This is the prerogative of the inter-action between instructions brought from the past and instruc-tions brought from the future—error and transgression. In revealing the past, we produce knowledge and its benefits, but we do not produce immortality. To achieve the latter we would have to master error, conquer experience, and live the future in the present. In our condition as matter, this might not be pos-sible. But all this is only a digression.

Religions will have predicted it. Psychoanalysis will have pointed to it. But it is biology that will discover the soul. Not a well-behaved soul but a deeply immoral soul.

This immoral soul is planted in the interstices of our pri-mordial instructions. It is the tool through which information, chemistry, and the organism produce themselves. Semen of creation, perhaps this is the seed we so desperately seek to sow.

NOTES

1. Martin Buber, *Ten Rungs* (New York: Schocken Books, 1947), p. 85.
2. Adapted from Martin Buber, *Tales of the Hasidim. Book Two: The Later Masters* (Schocken, 1961), p. 256.
3. Adapted from Martin Buber, *Tales of the Hasidim. Book One: The Early Masters* (Schocken, 1961), p. 291.
4. Adapted from Buber, *The Early Masters*, p. 89.
5. Howard Polsky, *Everyday Miracles: The Healing Wisdom of Hasidic Stories* (Jason Aronson, 1989).
6. Adapted from Buber, *The Later Masters*, p. 314.
7. Adapted from Buber, *The Early Masters*, p. 42.
8. Adapted from Buber, *The Later Masters*, p. 98.
9. Adin Steinsaltz, *The Golden Mean and the Horse Path* (Aleph Society, 1958).

10. Louis I. Newman, *Maggidim and Hasidim: Their Wisdom* (Bloch, 1962), p. 30.
11. Adapted from Buber, *The Later Masters*, p. 302.
12. Louis I. Newman, *The Hasidic Anthology* (Jason Aronson, 1987), p. 194.
13. Buber, *The Later Masters*, p. 257.
14. Adapted from Buber, *The Early Masters*, p. 292.
15. Ibid., p. 298.
16. Claude Lévi-Strauss, "The Structural Study of Myth," in *Structural Anthropology* (New York: Anchor Books, 1967).

Printed in the United States
By Bookmasters